The Age of Bluff

The Age of Bluff

PARADOX & AMBIGUITY
IN
RABELAIS & MONTAIGNE

Barbara C. Bowen

ILLINOIS STUDIES IN
LANGUAGE AND LITERATURE
62

University of Illinois Press
URBANA, CHICAGO, LONDON

© 1972 BY THE BOARD OF TRUSTEES OF THE UNIVERSITY OF ILLINOIS

MANUFACTURED IN THE UNITED STATES OF AMERICA

LIBRARY OF CONGRESS CATALOG CARD NO. 71-165041

ISBN 0-252-00212-1

In memory of my father, who taught me long ago
that it's all done with mirrors

Preface

This book is intended for friends, students, and scholars of French Renaissance literature who have read at least some of the works of Rabelais and Montaigne, preferably in French, and who are willing to consider with an open mind a critical approach rather different from what they are accustomed to. The first chapter sets out my method of approach, while the second and third consist mainly of detailed textual analysis and assume a reader willing to consult a specific edition of Rabelais or Montaigne as he goes along.

It is hoped that the footnotes will serve two purposes: to assure specialists that genuine evidence is being provided and essential debts acknowledged, and to encourage students to verify this evidence and to pursue the subject further. The general reader may cheerfully ignore them. The Bibliography includes only those works which have been used for, or which have particularly influenced, the present study.

I wish that I could here acknowledge my debt to all the colleagues and friends who will not need to read this book, because it is a direct result of their inspiration and encouragement. I can at least express my gratitude to those people whose approval and disapproval had the most influence on it: to Mrs. Tamara Root, whose strictures on Rabelais started me on the book; to Mr. Russell Witney, who as my research assistant struggled nobly with practical and critical problems related to the manuscript; and most especially to my colleagues Vincent E. Bowen, Stanley Gray, Will Moore, and Roy J. Nelson, whose invaluable comments and criticisms contributed so much to the book as it developed. They are in nowise responsible for the many imperfections remaining in it.

Contents

ABBREVIATIONS

BHR	*Bibliothèque d'Humanisme et Renaissance*
BRP	*Beiträge zur Romanischen Philologie*
CAIEF	*Cahiers de l'Association Internationale des Etudes Françaises*
CL	*Comparative Literature*
C.N.R.S.	Centre National de Recherche Scientifique
FS	*French Studies*
G.	Rabelais's *Gargantua*
MLQ	*Modern Language Quarterly*
MLR	*Modern Language Review*
MP	*Modern Philology*
NRF	*Nouvelle Revue Française*
P.	Rabelais's *Pantagruel*
P.U.F.	Presses Universitaires de France
Q.l.	Rabelais's *Quart livre*
RR	*Romanic Review*
S.E.D.E.S.	Société d'Edition d'Enseignement Supérieur
SFr	*Studi Francesi*
SP	*Studies in Philology*
SRLF	*Saggi e Ricerche di Letteratura Francese*
T.H.R.	Travaux d'Humanisme et Renaissance
T.l.	Rabelais's *Tiers livre*
T.L.F.	Textes Littéraires Français

The Age of Bluff

and why do we still all too often hear the good old bromides about Montaigne's "manuel de sagesse" (Armaingaud, in 1924) and Rabelais's "philosophie de la nature" (Saulnier, in 1967)? And why have there been no critical attempts to examine French Renaissance literature as a whole? Of course, a great deal of first-rate critical work has been done in the field, but the major studies, with the exception of some works on poetry, have been on individual authors, and there are no stimulating critical works on the French Renaissance as there are on Classicism and on the English Renaissance. The words "naïve," "primitive," "transitional," and "pre-Classical" are still constantly used, at least in print and I fear in the classroom as well, and the general impression persists that the sixteenth century was trying very hard to be Classical and was most successful when it managed it.

The purpose of this book is to encourage a better understanding of French Renaissance literature and to suggest that it does have a certain aesthetic unity, comparable in kind to the unity of outlook and technique shared by the major Classical writers. However, we have no hope of understanding the sixteenth century until we have put all direct comparisons with the seventeenth right out of our minds. Rabelais did not know that he would be followed by Molière, and if he had known, he would probably have found the prospect depressing. We must also endeavor to forget our conditioned expectations of what literature should be. We must not assume that the "best" book is the one with a firm plot line, symmetrically ordered structure, well-rounded characters, and unity of tone. The ideal attitude of mind, in fact, is one totally lacking in expectation of what a book is going to be like, but this is, of course, extremely difficult to achieve.

Perhaps the main reason that sixteenth-century literature has been so consistently misunderstood and underestimated is the tendency of scholars to streamline and synthesize the problems they are dealing with. We are all to some extent victims of what Empson has called the "either/or complex," and it is easy to see why: a scholar's whole training inclines him to tidying up problems, and if he were not a tidy-minded person, he would probably not have become a scholar. Unity is infinitely easier to grasp, and to talk about, than complexity, and it is very difficult indeed to talk about paradox and ambiguity without becoming paradoxical and ambiguous. But the most immediate necessity for a critical appreciation of this literature is to untidy it again after the excessive tidying-up to which it has been subjected since Sainte-Beuve: to examine objectively just what each writer is trying to do, and then to see what, if anything, these writers have in common.

Most of the present study will be devoted to Rabelais and Montaigne, but I should like to begin with a statement of my general thesis and a discussion of some of the evidence which led me to formulate it. Some of this evidence is in the form of causes (aspects of the literary and philosophical traditions behind the Renaissance literature we know), and some is in the form of effects (other Renaissance authors who share the outlook and/or techniques of the "major" writers of the period).

To return for a moment to the comparison with Classicism, I think the main difference between the two is that whereas the great writers of the seventeenth century were aiming to satisfy, aesthetically and intellectually, those of the sixteenth were seeking to stimulate. Rabelais and Montaigne, unlike as they are in many respects, both want to ask questions rather than answer them. They prod us, they demolish our card-houses of *idées reçues* and *expressions toutes faites,* they astonish and shock us by juxtaposition of different styles or themes, by swift changes in attitude which leave us puzzled. And whereas Classical literature might be characterized by concentration, by the paring away of inessentials to sharpen the focus on the essential, Renaissance literature is marked by the opposite: dispersion. Instead of concentrating on one essential aspect of a subject, a Renaissance writer is more likely to explore all its aspects, especially if they are contradictory, and to open up as many different perspectives as possible. This explains why, rather than symmetry, order, and balance, he will prefer paradox, enigma, argument, antithesis, and ambiguity—characteristics not just of the baroque but of the entire century.

Now my contention is that these characteristics, which, of course, refer both to the author's attitude of mind and to the literary techniques he uses, are aspects of a general intention, which is to disconcert the reader. There is, unfortunately, no noun meaning "the action of disconcerting," and "bluff" is the only general word I can find which can be used to include all the other terms I have mentioned. I am not using "bluff" in its card-playing context, where it implies deliberate deception and misleading. A Renaissance author is not normally bluffing in order to persuade his reader that a lie is the truth; the aim of his bluff is to make us stop and think, either about the subject under discussion or about the literary techniques being used. The reader's reaction, once he is alerted to the bluff process, may be one of shock, objection, or laughter, but he will in any case be disconcerted. Something unexpected has happened, causing him to revise a first impression, rethink a premise, or in some way change gear mentally.

"Bluff," then, will be used in this book to designate the result of one or more of the techniques mentioned—paradox, enigma, argument, antithesis, and ambiguity—used in a conscious effort to disconcert the reader. As we shall see, bluff varies from author to author and from page to page in any given author. The major technique may be ambiguity in Empson's sense, which is more common in poetry than in prose, or paradox and irony as in Donne and Shakespeare, or double bluff as in Rabelais. The main aim may be satire as often in Rabelais, moralizing as often in Shakespeare, or the reduction of the reader to a state of mental fog as often in Montaigne. But whatever the end and whatever the techniques used to this end, bluff is present in nearly all Renaissance writers and provides a unifying link between authors as different as Du Bellay and Sponde, Rabelais and Montaigne.

PROBLEMS OF COMPREHENSION

One very important reason that bluff has been ignored or under-estimated in the literature of this period is that readers tend to concentrate on the "modern" aspects of a Renaissance text and to reject as too difficult, or not really relevant, the obstacles to comprehension of it in its context. These obstacles can be of a linguistic or intellectual order, and I shall concentrate here on opportunities for paradox and ambiguity which are most likely to escape the uninformed modern reader. Clearly, in some of these cases ambiguity arises only from our lack of knowledge, and we must always distinguish carefully between ambiguity which is our fault as readers and ambiguity which was intended by the author. It is not possible to think oneself completely into the skin of a sixteenth-century reader, but it is quite possible to bear in mind what we know of his intellectual formation and background. We know a great deal, thanks to the patient research of generations of scholars, but we do not always use this specialized knowledge to attack problems in the most intelligent way.

Many factors contribute to basic differences in attitude between a sixteenth-century reader and a modern one. First and simplest, the sixteenth-century reader had to make far more effort than we do because he had no punctuation to guide him, or if there was punctuation, it simply indicated rhetorical pauses. The reader "created" the text as he went along, so that reading was a much more positive act for him than for us, who have simply to receive passively a text which has been already punctuated for us. Imagine the intellectual effort that must go into making sense of a passage like this one from the 1489 Levet edition of *Maistre Pierre Pathelin,* which is, moreover, in Gothic script:[1]

[1] Facsimile edition, T.L.F. (Geneva: Droz, 1953), b.ii v[0]; Barbara Bowen, ed., *Four Farces,* Blackwell's French Texts (Oxford: Basil Blackwell, 1967), pp. 69–70 (ll. 333-43).

Pathelin
Or et quoy doncques
or deable ie ny failly oncques
non or quil peult estre pendu
en dea il ne ma pas vendu
a mon mot ce a este au sien
mais il sera paie au mien
il luy fault or on le luy fourre
pleust a dieu quil ne fist que courre
sans cesser iusqua fin de paye
sainct iehan il feroit plus de voye
quil nya iusque a pampelune

Lack of formal punctuation can create genuine ambiguity—there is a passage in the same text (ll. 556–59) for which no punctuation seems altogether satisfactory. We should always bear in mind that in our modern editions the punctuation has been fixed for us by the editor, not by the author.[2]

Another important aspect of reading is often forgotten: at the time Rabelais wrote his first book, printed texts had only been available for two generations. His reader, conditioned by centuries of reading aloud and learning by heart, still pronounced the words, very possibly aloud, as he went along. This means that Rabelais and his contemporaries should be read aloud to be fully appreciated, and also that a writer's attitude to the language he was using was necessarily rather different.[3]

[2] The reader who is not familiar with sixteenth-century texts should look at Peter Rickard's anthology *La langue française au seizième siècle* (Cambridge: Cambridge University Press, 1968), which gives all texts in the original spelling, though with punctuation added.

[3] It would appear that even today a majority of scholars mentally pronounce words as they go along, at least when reading "work." Of thirty-three members of the University of Illinois French Department who answered a questionnaire on this subject, only five were convinced that all their reading was purely visual. For the influence of printing on reading habits, see W. J. Ong, *Ramus, Method and the Decay of Dialogue: From the Art of Discourse to the Art of Reason* (Cambridge, Mass.: Harvard University Press, 1958), and Marshall McLuhan, *The Gutenberg Galaxy: The Making of Typographic Man* (Toronto: University of Toronto Press, 1962).

Yet another linguistic problem concerns the Latin background of the Renaissance. We know that the humanists were brought up on Latin, but we do not always realize how well that language is suited to epigram and antithesis. Certainly, it is much easier to avoid ambiguity in Latin than in French or English because of its grammatical structure, but this fact itself presents serious problems in translation, especially to people who have been brought up to think in Latin. We grew up in an atmosphere of quotation from the Bible and Shakespeare, which had a definite influence on our style and thought processes. The sixteenth century was similarly soaked in "adages" and "apothegms" from the Classics, which must also have influenced their mental habits. If you translate "Oderint dum metuant" (Erasmus, *Adages,* II, ix, lxii), or "Dulce bellum inexpertis" (IV, i, i), you can render the meaning but not the symmetrical and economical construction characteristic of the Latin. These problems are not difficult to deal with once one is aware of them, but too often they are not borne in mind at all. The same applies to problems of vocabulary and syntax—Huguet's dictionary will tell you what *pourtant, si,* and *garce* meant at this time, but you will not look them up unless it has occurred to you that their meaning may have changed over the centuries.

Far greater obstacles arise when we come to the question of sources. The average Anglo-Saxon reader today has not had a Classical education, and even if he has, it may not be a great deal of help. He may know Cicero, Virgil, Ovid, and Caesar; he is most unlikely to have read Diogenes Laertius, Macrobius, the Church Fathers, the fifteenth-century Italian philosophers, and Erasmus. Clearly, the general reader cannot possibly remedy all the lacunae in his education in order to fill these gaps, but he can, once again, be aware of the problem. And he can be aware that a great deal of the intellectual background of the sixteenth century is concerned with paradox, ambiguity, or dialectic. Let us glance briefly at some of the best-known authors and genres which influenced the Renaissance way of thought.

We must not forget, first of all, medieval biblical exegesis on at
least four different levels. For centuries any biblical text was interpreted literally *and* tropologically *and* allegorically *and* anagogically,
and Renaissance authors are still "allegorizing" Virgil and Ovid.[4] This
procedure is clearly the exact opposite of the either/or complex; a
reader so trained will *expect* a text to be valid on several different
levels and will not feel the need to single out any one interpretation
over the others.

Many of the most influential Classical writers had dealt in paradox and irony for varying reasons. Plato's dialogues use dialectical
arguments, paradox, and irony for didactic purposes. Many of Socrates'
arguments have no firm conclusion, and his use of irony and mockery
was even more familiar in the Renaissance than it is now.[5] Lucian's
dialogues use paradox, and in particular the paradoxical eulogy, for
satirical purposes, and Cicero's *Paradoxa* treats ethical paradoxes already discussed by the Stoics. Ovid's *Metamorphoses* induces a feeling
of uneasiness about a natural world in which nothing is what it
seems. And Plutarch's *Lives* is based on the paradox of resemblance
between a famous Greek life and a famous Roman one.

Closer in time to the Renaissance, the general literary atmosphere
is more inclined yet to paradox and argument. Among the most
popular medieval genres are the *débat,* the *tençon,* and the *jeu-parti,*
and toward the Renaissance period the riddle and the enigma.[6] The
paradox becomes a literary genre in its own right, especially in Italy
and England. The *Capitoli* of Francesco Berni (1537), with its praise
of eels, debts, chamber-pots, jelly, and needles, and the *Paradossi* of
Ortensio Lando (1543, translated by Charles Estienne in 1553), which

[4] See Harry Caplan, "The Four Senses of Scriptural Interpretation and the Medieval
Theory of Preaching," *Speculum* IV (1929), 282–90. There is an entertaining illustration of this method in T. H. White's *The Sword in the Stone,* at the end of ch. XIX.
[5] See below, Chapter II, p. 53, and Chapter III, p. 126.
[6] See V.-L. Saulnier, "Proverbe et paradoxe du XVe au XVIe siècle. Un aspect majeur
de l'antithèse: Moyen Age–Renaissance," in *Pensée humaniste et tradition chrétienne
aux XVe et XVIe siècles,* Colloques Internationaux du C.N.R.S. (Paris: C.N.R.S., 1950);
and Michele De Filippis, *The Literary Riddle in Italy to the End of the Sixteenth
Century* (Berkeley and Los Angeles: University of California Press, 1948).

maintains that ignorance is more excellent than wisdom, drunkenness than sobriety, and woman than man, were known throughout Europe.[7] Rosalie Colie's book, among many other critical works, shows how important paradox is in English Renaissance literature, and she quotes many works in this genre, like *The Prayse of Nothing* (1625?), Michael Maier's *Jocus severus* (1617), and Ralph Venning's *Orthodox Paradoxes* (1647).

The standard paradox is undoubtedly less common in France, but there are enough examples to show that it was recognized as a literary form. Charles Estienne's translation or, rather, adaptation of Lando is entitled *Paradoxes, ce sont propos contre la commune opinion,* and we do have a few works with titles like *Paradoxe apologétique, ou il est fidèlement demonstré que la femme est beaucoup plus parfaicte que l'homme en toute action de vertu* (by Alexandre de Pont-Aymery, 1598). It is now recognized that many of the works classified under the famous *querelle des femmes,* and taken by Abel Lefranc as serious polemics, are exercises in paradox. Jean Nevizan's *Sylvae nuptialis libri sex,* published in 1540, comprises two books against marriage and two in favor of it. Bertrand de La Borderie's *Amye de court* (1542), in spite of its title, is a cynical portrait of woman which denies her any noble qualities. The anonymous *Louenge des femmes* (1551), probably by Sebillet,[8] is an antifeminist work, and Sebillet also wrote a *Paradoxe contre l'amour* (1581). And so on.

The case of Cornelius Agrippa is still disputed: why did he write a textbook of occult philosophy (*De occulta philosophia,* first printed in its complete version in 1533) and a condemnation of all philosophy

[7] See N. N. Condeescu, "Le paradoxe bernesque dans la littérature française de la Renaissance," *BRP* II (1963), 27–51; and Rosalie I. Colie, *Paradoxia Epidemica: The Renaissance Tradition of Paradox* (Princeton, N.J.: Princeton University Press, 1966). For Lando, see Warner G. Rice, "The *Paradossi* of Ortensio Lando," in *Essays and Studies in English and Comparative Literature by Members of the English Department of the University of Michigan* (Ann Arbor: University of Michigan Press, 1932), pp. 59–74.

[8] See M. A. Screech, "An Interpretation of the Querelle des Amyes," *BHR* XXI (1959), 103–30.

(*De incertitudine et vanitate scientiarum,* first published in 1530)?
The reason is probably that the second is a paradox, as the title of
the French translation of 1608 by Louis Turquet de Mayerne suggests:
Paradoxe sur l'incertitude, vanité et abus des sciences. Agrippa's contribution to the *querelle des femmes* is the *De nobilitate et praecel-
lentia foeminei sexus* (1529), which so exaggerates the praise of
women that the most ardent feminist could not take it seriously. The
full title of the *De incertitudine* includes the word *declamatio,* and
Agrippa tells us himself that a *declamatio* is not to be taken at face
value: "Proinde declamatio non judicat, non dogmatizat sed . . . alia
joco, alia serio, alia false, alia saevere dicit . . . quaedam vera, quaedam falsa, quaedam dubia pronunciat . . . multa invalida argumenta
adducit. . . ."[9] The book was written as a deliberate paradox, and the
contradictions between it and the *De occulta philosophia* need not
shock us. There is a parallel case in Boaystuau; his *Le theatre du
monde, ou il est faict un ample discours des miseres de l'homme* was
bound in 1561 with his *Bref discours de l'excellence et dignité de
l'homme,* which contradicts it in every aspect.[10]

　　Poetic paradoxes are frequent, and Colie quotes the most famous,
Jean Passerat's Latin *Nihil.* The paradoxical encomium is common
also in prose, though seldom as common as in Rabelais's *Tiers livre,*
where we have satirical eulogies of debtors (chs. 3–4), codpieces (ch.
8), cuckoldry (ch. 28), and Pantagruélion (chs. 50–52; see below,
Chapter II). The whole subject of the paradox as a minor literary
genre in France has not yet received the treatment it deserves, but
these few examples should suffice to show that it does exist as part
of the general atmosphere we are discussing.

　　And it is this general atmosphere which explains the immense
success of Erasmus's *Praise of Folly* (1509), a standard paradox sub-

[9] *Henrici Cornelii Agrippae . . . apologia adversus calumnias propter declamationem
de vanitate scientiarum . . .* (1533), ch. XLII; quoted in M. A. Screech, "Rabelais, De
Billon and Erasmus," *BHR* XIII (1951), 241–65.
[10] The information in George Boas, *The Happy Beast in French Thought of the
Seventeenth Century* (Baltimore: Johns Hopkins Press, 1933), pp. 15–22, is misleading
—they are not two halves of the same work but two separate works.

ject which his genius transforms into a literary masterpiece. The influence of Erasmus on the French Renaissance has been noted by many critics, but they have failed in most cases to point out the importance of paradox in his work.[11] Apart from *The Praise of Folly*, in which paradox and irony are all-important, French writers had read the *Colloquies*, where argument and satire are used to make a moral point, and the *Adages*. In his introduction to the *Adages* Erasmus gives this definition, among others, of an adage or proverb: "Proverbium est sermo rem manifestam obscuritate tegens."[12] This puts the emphasis squarely on the "bluff" aspect of a proverb, which will essentially hide what is normally clear, so that the reader must unravel the language to get at the *rem manifestam*.[13] In many of the longest adages Erasmus delights in paradox, most strikingly perhaps in "Sileni Alcibiadis" (III, iii, i), in which he uses Christ as an illustration of the Silenus image applied to Socrates in the *Symposium*.[14] The playful attitude he often takes toward his reader was certainly not lost on Rabelais and Montaigne.

Even this brief glance at the literary background, then, shows the importance of paradox, irony, and ambiguity for Renaissance writers. There may well be more practical reasons for their use. In times of political and religious unrest allegory is often popular, as *Les lettres persanes* and Sartre's *Les mouches* show clearly enough. Fear of the Sorbonne, the king, or the Inquisition may encourage a writer to propound his views on religion in a farcical context (Rabelais and perhaps Des Périers) or to hide his views on a dangerous

11 With the exception of Sister M. Geraldine, C.S.J., "Erasmus and the Tradition of Paradox," *SP* LXI (1964), 41–63.

12 *Desiderii Erasmi Roterodami opera omnia . . . tomus secundus, complectens adagia* (Leiden, 1703; republished, London: Gregg Press, 1962), p. 1.

13 For this double function of paradox, see A. E. Malloch, "The Techniques and Function of the Renaissance Paradox," *SP* LIII (1956), 191–203.

14 Toward the end of the *Symposium* (XXXII) Alcibiades compares Socrates to a trick statuette which is really a box. It looks like the statue of an ugly Silenus but, when opened, contains the statue of a god. Similarly, Socrates is ugly in body, but his soul contains incomparable wisdom. There is an English translation of this adage and several others in Margaret Mann Phillips, *The "Adages" of Erasmus: A Study with Translations* (Cambridge: Cambridge University Press, 1964).

subject in a discussion of something else (Montaigne in "Des boy-teux"). While we are on the subject of contexts, another important aspect of Renaissance literature should be borne in mind: the lack of a clear dividing line between fiction and nonfiction. On the one hand, we have philosophical dialogues between fictional characters in a fictional setting (see below); on the other Rabelais's fictional epic, which contains not only discussion of contemporary religious controversy but long passages on, say, scholastic medical theory (*T.l.*, ch. 4) which might have been lifted straight from a textbook. This should strike a modern reader as very odd, though not necessarily as ambiguous.

But we have by no means exhausted the reasons for a sixteenth-century writer's delight in paradox. Not only his reading but his whole education encouraged this, for he had been trained in the age-old scholastic tradition in which formal argument played a very large part. We laugh heartily today at the medieval disputes over how many angels could stand on the head of a pin, but we forget that for the disputants what mattered was not the conclusion to be reached but the argument to be used. The same exercise survives today in the British school debating societies, which expend great effort and elo-quence on subjects like "That Marks and Spencer have contributed more to the development of civilization than either Marx or Spenser." No one is interested in the conclusion, and the audience votes not for the most truthful speaker but for the most ingenious and eloquent one. Medieval philosophers, moreover, often seem to take a perverse delight in ambiguous terms which leave the burden of interpretation on the reader. Ockham's use of words like *figura, nomen,* and *passio* is often quite unclear to the modern reader, and, of course, *logos* al-ready had an enormous range of meanings in ancient Greek phi-losophy.

The tradition of logic and rhetoric is dead today, so dead that we tend to forget that it ever existed. This is unfortunate, because we can-not begin to understand the sixteenth century until we have realized how much most of its literature owes to this tradition. The interested student should consult a work on rhetoric [15] and read Ramus's *Dialectique* of 1555,[16] which will give him a fair idea of the scope of the problem. There are three basic principles to be borne in mind here. First, an argument had to be developed in a standard way according to the rules of logic, and the moral validity of an argument was not to be confused with its logical validity. The only rule most people retain about syllogisms is the fallacy produced by the undistributed middle, which invalidates such arguments as "Cats like fish; Socrates likes fish; therefore Socrates is a cat." There are, in fact, a great many different kinds of syllogisms, all with their own rules; moreover, any syllogism is logically valid if it conforms to the rules, even if the premises are completely false. Logic as a discipline was not usually intended to be a way of discovering new philosophical truths but simply a method of expounding with irrefutable clarity truths already known.

Second, the whole process of argument by this method is based on the use of the commonplace or *topos*. *Topoi* may be conveniently divided into two categories, philosophical and literary, but the principle is the same in each case. Every would-be writer, from the traditionally taught schoolboy to the humanist, had a commonplace book in which he recorded, under separate headings, stock arguments and literary ornaments from Classical writers, intended for his own future use.[17] If philosophical, a *topos* might concern the essentially fluctuating nature of things (Erasmus, *Adages,* I, vii, lxiii: "Omnium rerum vicissitudo est"). This *topos* goes back at least to Heraclitus, who said that you cannot step twice into the same river, and is copiously developed by Montaigne in the final pages of the "Apologie de Raymond Sebond." If literary, the *topos* might be a list of essential items to be

---

[15] See, for instance, William G. Crane, *Wit and Rhetoric in the Renaissance: The Formal Basis of Elizabethan Prose Style* (New York: Columbia University Press, 1937).

[16] Ed. Michel Dassonville, T.H.R., vol. LXVII (Geneva: Droz, 1964).

[17] See Paul Porteau, *Montaigne et la vie pédagogique de son temps* (Paris: Droz, 1935).

used in describing a spring morning, or the *carpe diem* commonplace
(Horace, *Odes*, I, 7) used by Ronsard in "Mignonne, allons voir" and
by Herrick in "Gather ye rosebuds while ye may."

The third and most important point is a consequence of the other
two and cannot be overemphasized: originality is not prized by the
sixteenth century. In the *Defense et illustration de la langue françoyse*
Du Bellay is not so much concerned with originality of subject matter as with correctness and elegance of treatment and the necessity to
equal (but not surpass) the Ancients. Since the Romantic period
poetry has been so exclusively personal that we have forgotten how to
evaluate nonpersonal poetry. It is very doubtful that the Pleiade poets
were interested in people at all—several of them had imaginary mis-
tresses, and Ronsard was probably never in love with Hélène.[18] They
were simply trying to elaborate in different ways the stock subjects
of poetry since Classical times.

The same applies in prose. Rabelais takes over a cast of characters from a mock epic and lifts whole passages from earlier authors,
the *conteurs* retell stories which everyone knows, and Montaigne lines
up the stock scholastic arguments for and against drunkenness, suicide, or repentance. Of course, any great writer will be original, but
we must not expect originality to be his main interest, and we must
not make it our main criterion in evaluating his work.

There are many other obstacles to our understanding which also
need elucidation. In the area of intellectual sources we should not
forget the enthusiasm for occult fields of learning, which confuses us
but which encouraged Renaissance writers to be mysterious and symbolic. Most of them were interested in one or more of the following:
the Cabala, Hermetic philosophy, astrology, alchemy, arithmosophy
(number symbolism), abstruse methods of divination, emblems, and
heraldry. Here it is not the nineteenth century which leads us astray
but the eighteenth. We are still convinced, officially at least, that the

---

[18] See Fernand Desonay, *Ronsard, poète de l'amour*, 3 vols. (Brussels: Palais des
Académies, 1952–59).

universe and our place in it are to be explained rationally. The six-teenth century was not so convinced, and instead of dismissing their beliefs as naïve, we should make an effort to understand them. They *knew* that ghosts walked, that comets were portents, that Virgil had foretold the birth of Christ, that the physical and metaphysical parts of the universe corresponded as parts of a pattern laid out by God. If you never knock on wood and have never met anyone who believes in ESP, second sight, horoscopes, or Groundhog Day, then you may have the right to criticize this mentality as "primitive."

BLUFF IN ACTION

All of these problems just discussed—reading, the influence of Latin, Classical sources, medieval and Renaissance literary genres, edu-cational practice, the tradition of logic and rhetoric, and love of obscure learning—point in the same direction. They demonstrate that the Renaissance writer had been brought up on paradox, educated by means of it, entertained by reading it. It would therefore be very surprising indeed if he did not naturally exploit it in his writing. In fact, there are very few writers who are not interested in paradox, and a very large number of them use the techniques of paradox in the service of what I am calling bluff, that is to say, with the intention of confusing and disconcerting the reader.

Now it is clear that paradox does not always imply bluff. In poetry, especially, paradox is normally used not to disconcert the reader but for its own sake. There is no doubt that Renaissance poets are par-ticularly attracted by paradox, but until quite late in the century the element of bluff is absent. Sponde, like Villon in the previous cen-tury,[19] uses techniques which startle and shock the reader, whereas

[19] See the remarkable study by David Kuhn, *La poétique de François Villon* (Paris: Colin, 1967).

Du Bellay, for instance, tends to disguise his paradoxes. Take, for example, the third sonnet of the *Antiquitez de Rome:*

> Nouveau venu qui cherches Rome en Rome,
> Et rien de Rome en Rome n'apperçois,
> Ces vieux palais, ces vieux arcz que tu vois,
> Et ces vieux murs, c'est ce que Rome on nomme.
> Voy quel orgueil, quelle ruine: et comme
> Celle qui mist le monde sous ses loix
> Pour donter tout, se donta quelquefois,
> Et devint proye au temps, qui tout consomme.
> Rome de Rome est le seul monument,
> Et Rome Rome a vaincu seulement;
> Le Tybre seul, qui vers la mer s'enfuit,
> Reste de Rome. O mondaine inconstance!
> Ce qui est ferme, est par le temps destruit,
> Et ce qui fuit, au temps fait resistence.[20]

This is a remarkably close translation of a Latin poem, perhaps by Jean Vitalis:

> Qui Romam in media quaeris, novus advena, Roma,
> Et Romae in Roma nil reperis in media,
> Aspice murorum mures, praeruptaque saxa,
> Obrutaque horrendi vasta theatra situ.
> Haec sunt Roma: viden' velut ipsa cadavera tantae
> Urbis adhuc spirent imperiosa minas?
> Vicit ut haec mundum, visa est se vincere: vicit,
> A se non victum ne quid in orbe foret.
> Nunc victa in Roma Roma illa invicta sepulta est,
> Atque eadem victrix victaque Roma fuit.
> Albula Romani restat nunc nominis index:

---

[20] Both texts are from Joachim Du Bellay, *Les regrets et autres oeuvres poëtiques,* ed. J. Jolliffe and M. A. Screech, T.L.F. (Geneva: Droz, 1966), p. 275. A very different approach from mine can be found in André Six, *"Explication française:* Du Bellay, *Antiquités de Rome*—Sonnet III," *Romance Notes* VIII (Spring 1967), 281–84.

Quin etiam rapidis fertur in aequor aquis.
Disce hinc quid possit Fortuna. Immota labascunt,
Et quae perpetuo sunt agitata manent.

Now this source is based on two philosophical commonplaces: the destructive power of time ("Tempus edax rerum," Ovid, *Metamorphoses*, XV, 234, or "Fugit inreparabile tempus," Virgil, *Georgics*, iii, 284) and the impermanence of everything (Erasmus's "Omnium rerum vicissitudo est," already mentioned). The main stylistic interest of the Latin is the play on forms of *vincere* and *se vincere*, and the author does not specifically mention time. What does Du Bellay do with this? He abandons the repetition of *vincere* and replaces it with a series of different verbs, and he also abandons the related *topos* of Fortuna. He adds the adjective *vieux*, repeated three times in lines 3–4 to give it a pejorative note, and balances it with three uses of *temps* (ll. 8, 13, 14) which generalize the original *topos*. He retains the nine references to Rome but incorporates the word into an astonishing sound structure based on [ɔ m] and related nasals. So far he seems to be using less, rather than more, paradox than the source. But he has also added a reflection on the deceptiveness of names: he translates *Haec sunt Roma* by *c'est ce que Rome on nomme*. In particular, he has introduced an ambiguity which is not present in the Latin at all. This ambiguity begins with the repetition of *vieux*, which ought not, in the context, to be pejorative. Are not the ruins admired because they are old and because they remind us of "le bon vieux temps" which was so much nobler and more virtuous than the present day? But the repetition itself raises doubts, and by the end of the poem the reader is asking, did Rome ever exist? What we call Rome (l. 4) is the only monument of the real Rome (l. 9) and is just a ruin (l. 5); but since the essence of the real Rome was pride (l. 5), based on an invincibility (l. 6) which turned out to be illusory, is not our whole concept of Rome at fault? So line 9 acquires a note of deeper disillusionment: the present Rome, sad as it is, is perhaps a *fitting* monument to the "real" Rome.

Du Bellay's intention is not, apparently, to shock the reader but to point out all the ambiguity inherent in the original paradox. The poem is thus more fundamentally a paradox than its source; in the Latin poem Rome has gone forever, but in the French poem it never was.

It is especially interesting to compare Du Bellay with Sponde. They share several themes, especially time and death, and no one would dispute Sponde's interest in paradox, since he is generally recognized as baroque. But apart from the paradoxical and antithetical subject matter of his poems and the baroque qualities of their images, they have a deliberately disconcerting form which exemplifies what I am calling bluff. A good example is the well-known final "Sonnet de la mort":

> Tout s'enfle contre moy, tout m'assaut, tout me tente,
> Et le Monde, et la Chair, et l'Ange revolté,
> Dont l'onde, dont l'effort, dont le charme inventé
> Et m'abysme, Seigneur, et m'esbranle, et m'enchante.
> Quelle nef, quel appuy, quelle oreille dormante,
> Sans peril, sans tomber, et sans estre enchanté,
> Me donras-tu? Ton Temple où vit ta Saincteté,
> Ton invincible main, et ta voix si constante.
> Et quoy? mon Dieu, je sens combattre maintesfois
> Encor avec ton Temple, et ta main, et ta voix,
> Cest Ange revolté, ceste chair, et ce Monde.
> Mais ton Temple pourtant, ta main, ta voix sera
> La nef, l'appuy, l'oreille, où ce charme perdra,
> Où mourra cest effort, où se rompra ceste onde.[21]

21 This is the 1588 text reproduced by Schmidt in *Poètes du XVIe siècle* (see next note), p. 898, except that I have replaced the comma at the end of line 4 with a period. The 1599 text, in the Boase and Ruchon edition, has a question mark at the end of line 8 and *perdra* instead of *rompra* in the last line. There is an interesting analysis of this poem by Claude-Gilbert Dubois, "Autour d'un sonnet de Sponde: recherche de l'élément baroque," *L'Information Littéraire* (Mar.–Apr. 1967), pp. 86–92.

This is a *sonnet rapporté,* but slightly asymmetrical, and the most astonishing thing about it is the richness of metaphor packed into it.[22] A sonnet is already a fairly rigid form, and a *sonnet rapporté* is so much more rigid that there are very few examples of the genre which are even poetically adequate. Sponde's is successful largely because of his constant effort to surprise and disconcert the reader. Incidentally, a *sonnet rapporté* is often considered merely an intellectual tour de force, but here the tripartite division is ideally suited to the subject matter: the traditional threefold temptation (world, flesh, devil) is resisted with the help of God, who is three in one.

In the first line the three verbs prepare us for the three nouns in line 2 and warn us that the poem needs to be read "vertically." But each verb has a very different connotation, and by the end of the first quatrain the poet is in three different relationships with the world, the flesh, and the devil: the World is a wave which swells up and drowns him, the Flesh is an attacking army whose effort makes him waver, and the Devil is a tempter who casts a spell on him. The first two images are quite orthodox, but the devil, orthodox enough in lines 1 and 2, is gradually turning into a much more secular enchanter in lines 3 and 4. Line 5 has two ambiguous elements. *Nef* can be a ship, but it can also be the nave of a church and so prepares us for *Temple* in line 7. And *oreille dormante* transforms the devil from a biblical tempter into something more like the Sirens of the *Odyssey,* whom one could only resist if asleep or deaf. Line 6 is symmetrical, except that *peril* and *tomber* develop their respective images whereas *enchanté* repeats *enchante* in line 4, but in line 7 the symmetry is suddenly broken. The replies do not correspond to the poet's anguished questions, either in position or in meaning. *Temple* is at first sight a surprising protection against a wave, but it has been prepared for by

---

[22] A *sonnet rapporté* normally has a tripartite line division, and the general effect is of being written in three columns so that it can be read vertically as well as horizontally. The classic example of the genre is the second sonnet of Jodelle's *Amours* ("Des astres, des forests, et d'Acheron l'honneur," in A.-M. Schmidt, ed., *Poètes du XVIe siècle* (Paris: Bibliothèque de la Pléiade, 1953), p. 711).

nef and reminds us that we are not talking about a real wave but about the World, from which a church is clearly the best escape. *Main* is perfectly logical as an *appuy* against the danger of falling, but *voix* is very odd, since it corresponds to *oreille* in line 5, and since a voice seems a curious protection against another voice. A moment's reflection tells us that God's *constante* voice will be stronger than the tempting voice of the devil, whose *charme* is *inventé,* but *voix* is at first sight disconcerting. Moreover, *main* and *voix,* being both connected with the human body, give us second thoughts about *Temple,* which can mean temple in the anatomical sense. This would give us a sudden picture of God reduced to human proportions. This sentence is also strikingly asymmetrical after the rigid structure which precedes it—*Temple* is modified by a clause which permits a nice alliteration of *t*'s, *main* by a preceding adjective, and *voix* by *si* and a following adjective.

The poem could be complete at the end of line 8, since a solution has apparently been given to the poet's problem. Sponde sets it in motion again with a brief interjection and an explanation that the apparent solution of line 8 was an illusion—in spite of God's help the struggle continues. In line 10 he returns to the tripartite line division but in line 11 reverses the order, so that the original *Monde-Temple, Chair-main,* and *Ange revolté-voix* combat now becomes *Ange revolté-Temple, Chair-main,* and *Monde-voix.* The final tercet contains the genuine solution to the poet's conflict, and this solution is unexpected. God's help will not abolish the conflict, as the poet was requesting in lines 5–7, but it will enable him to stand firm against the attacks of the world, the flesh, and the devil. This tercet contains the same disconcerting assimilation of *voix* to *oreille,* and the last two lines reverse the order of terms once more, so that instead of reading down as in the first quatrain, we read along and connect *oreille* with *charme, appuy* with *effort,* and *nef* with *onde* as the logic of the poem seems to require.

The major effects of this poem, then, are those of sudden departure from the expected logic or imagery of a *sonnet rapporté*. A final disconcerting aspect is that whereas within the poem the water image is attached to only one of the three elements, the poem itself is constructed to resemble a wave; it swells at the beginning, subsides in lines 7–8, swells again, and finally breaks on the beach in the lengthening clauses and sounds of the last line.

I hope this brief analysis has shown how striking the differences are between the two poets. Du Bellay uses, and delights in, paradox, but he subordinates it to a harmonious overall effect, while Sponde does the opposite: his paradoxical twists and turns are designed to destroy harmony and to jolt his reader into a new awareness, both of the subject matter of the poem and of its structure. Between Du Bellay and Sponde the poem has become self-conscious.

There are many other poets of the period, including Ronsard, who exploit paradox in different ways and with different effects. I have chosen not to pursue paradox in poetry for two reasons. First, poetry, at least since Empson, is expected to deal in paradox and ambiguity, whereas prose is not, at least not to the same extent. Second, the subject of paradox in French Renaissance poetry has been dealt with in several critical works, whereas the prose works of the period have in many cases not been discussed at all.[23] And these prose works contain some of the most interesting examples of Renaissance bluff in action. The masters of the art are Rabelais and Montaigne, whom I shall be discussing at length in later chapters, but there is a great deal of interesting evidence among far less well-known writers.

One subject which has been almost totally neglected by critics is the prevalence of dialogue in the sixteenth century.[24] Dialogue does not necessarily entail bluff any more than poetry does; Erasmus's

[23] See, for instance, Jean-Claude Margolin, "*L'Hymne de l'or* et son ambiguité," *BHR* XXVIII (1966), 271–93; Gérard Genette, *Figures* (Paris: Seuil, 1966); and numerous works on the baroque.

[24] See the unpublished thesis by Mustapha Benouis, "Le dialogue intellectuel en France au XVIe siècle" (University of Illinois, Urbana, 1970).

colloquy "Naufragium," for instance, contains irony and satire but
no bluff.[25] The author's attitude to his subject and to the reader is
perfectly straightforward, and the moral is plain and direct. Plato's
dialogues, on the other hand, use bluff a good deal. Socrates leads his
interlocutor into an argument which appears valid and which suddenly turns out to be invalid, or pretends to be supporting the point
of view he will eventually refute, or fails to conclude and leaves the
whole discussion hanging on a question mark. Plato's influence on
the Renaissance was considerable, and the technique of his dialogues
was not lost on writers like De Brués and Montaigne.

It is very difficult to treat dialogue as a genre because the many
examples we have are so different in subject matter and technique.
Louis Le Caron's *Dialogues* are expository, intended at the same time
as publicity for philosophy as an intellectual attitude and as debunk-
ing of popular and unintelligent views on scientific subjects.[26] They
are undoubtedly dull, but Pontus de Tyard manages to make the
same technique interesting by using interlocutors who have personality
and an individual viewpoint.[27] This type of dialogue owes a good
deal to the encyclopaedic compendium of the Middle Ages and
generally consists of a summary of scientific knowledge of the time
or a rehash of theories on the soul and God according to ancient
philosophers. Little if any bluff is involved here or in the delightful
polemic dialogues of Henri Estienne, which preserve for posterity the
eccentricities of Italianate speech toward the end of the century.[28]
Estienne's dialogues are more genuinely dramatic than those of Le
Caron and Tyard, but he is too heavy-handed to indulge in bluff, pre-
ferring to overwhelm his reader with the full force of his argument.

[25] *The Colloquies of Erasmus: A New Translation,* tr. Craig R. Thompson (Chicago:
University of Chicago Press, 1965).
[26] *Les dialogues de Loys Le Caron* (Paris, 1556). There is no modern edition.
[27] *The Universe of Pontus de Tyard: A Critical Edition of L'univers,* ed. John C. Lapp
(Ithaca, N.Y.: Cornell University Press, 1950). Tyard's other dialogues are listed in
the introduction.
[28] Henri Estienne, *Deux dialogues du nouveau langage françois italianizé,* ed.
P. Ristelhuber, 2 vols. (Paris, 1885).

But there are many dialogue writers who do use bluff in very different ways. Palissy's *Recepte veritable* (1563) purports to be a description of how to lay out a garden and is, in fact, a plea for the Reformed religion.[29] The *Heptameron* of Marguerite de Navarre is a good collection of stories, but critics have generally agreed that the main function of the stories is to serve as pretext for debate among the *devisants* on the nature of love, woman's place in society, and other moral and ethical problems. We are quite sure today which is Marguerite's own point of view because we have many other works by her which are not ambiguous, but if only the *Heptameron* had come down to us, and if we did not know that the author was a woman, should we be so sure? The frequent debates between Hircan, who believes that woman is an instrument of pleasure for man and nothing more, and the neo-Platonist Dagoucin, who believes in chaste and reverent love from a distance, are never really concluded. Stories are told to illustrate both points of view, and certainly more stories are on the side of true love than against it, but the discussions of the *devisants* do not come to a firm conclusion. It is possible that if Marguerite had finished the book, she would have clarified her point of view, but it is also possible that the argument itself interests her more than the conclusion.

Among the writers of dialogue as a genre, one of the least known and most interesting is Guy de Brués, author of *Les dialogues de Guy de Brués, contre les nouveaux académiciens, que tout ne consiste point en opinion* (1557).[30] Curiously enough, it is rare for a dialogue writer to imitate Plato's didactic method, but this is what De Brués does. He sets out to destroy the skeptical point of view on mainly common-sense grounds: if everything is opinion, then nothing can be known, which is for him a defeatist attitude as well as a nonreligious one. I see no reason to doubt De Brués's sincerity here, although his modern

---

[29] In *Les oeuvres de Bernard Palissy,* ed. Anatole France (Paris, 1880).
[30] Ed. Panos Paul Morphos (Baltimore: Johns Hopkins Press, 1953). Page references in the text are to this edition.

editor, following Busson, attempts to do so.[31] In order to destroy the
skeptical point of view, he first allows an interlocutor to expound and
defend it at great length, and the final conversion to right thinking
is rendered all the more dramatic by the tenacity of his previous
resistance.

The book contains three dialogues, on epistemology, ethics, and
the law respectively, and a brief examination of the first will show how
De Brués uses bluff to assist the presentation of a basically serious
thesis. To begin with, he uses as interlocutors real people: Ronsard,
Baïf, Aubert (a well-known lawyer and humanist), and Nicot (also
well known, a lawyer and diplomat, who introduced tobacco into
France and gave his name to nicotine). Modern critics tend to assume
that portraits of real people in works of fiction must be true to life,
but why should they be? In Le Caron's dialogue "Valton" one of the
interlocutors is Rabelais, but the views he expresses are quite obviously
Le Caron's own. Certainly Ronsard's quarrel with Baïf, which we
know about from other sources, is mentioned here, and certainly
Ronsard quotes from his own poems, but there is no evidence that
the opinions here expressed are specifically or exclusively those of any
particular person. Rather, De Brués is using real names to establish
verisimilitude and because he hopes more people will read a book
which is apparently "about" well-known contemporary characters.

But verisimilitude created by the use of these names is contradicted by the setting of the scene. De Brués describes a sunny meadow
and a stream running through the shade of a willow tree—elements which had become traditional in literature and are, of course,
not unknown in real life, but which to a humanist would recall in
particular the opening of Plato's *Phaedrus*. So the real-life aspect
(names of the interlocutors) is at once counterbalanced by a literary
aspect, leaving the alert reader a little puzzled at the outset.

---

[31] Henri Busson, *Le rationalisme dans la littérature française de la Renaissance*
(*1533–1601*), rev. ed. (Paris: Vrin, 1957).

The subject matter of this first dialogue, mainly a debate between Ronsard and Baïf with brief interventions by the other two, is the age-old philosophical quarrel about whether anything can be known. This argument is often taken as the one which basically divides Plato from Aristotle, but Ronsard and Baïf use evidence from any philosopher who supports their point of view. Ronsard uses Cicero to back Aristotle's view that laws are based on reason, not on opinion (p. 99), while elsewhere Baïf relies on Cicero to oppose Ronsard's support of Aristotle. Aubert concludes on p. 161 that Aristotle and Plato are not fundamentally opposed, a typically Renaissance view. The discussion ranges over many subjects—the soul, law, the reliability of our senses, medicine, dialectic, geometry, and astronomy— providing at the same time an epistemological argument and a résumé of contemporary knowledge in different domains. What distinguishes this dialogue from others on the same subject is the playful tone which De Brués very cleverly introduces without undermining the serious import of the discussion.

This dialogue occupies pp. 93–180 of the Morphos edition, and as early as p. 100 there are indications that Baïf's point of view, "en tout n'y a qu'opinion," is not in fact what he believes. Ronsard says "Par ton discours je congnois assez que tu n'ignores pas quelle est la plus saine et meilleure opinion, mais tu t'esbas comme tu as promis à desbatre contre la verité." On p. 101 Baïf admits it: "Il me plaist de le dire par maniere de dispute." There are half a dozen other references to the fact that Baïf is playing a part, setting up an artificial thesis for Ronsard to demolish. However, Baïf does a good job of defending the thesis in question. Not until p. 167 does he begin to give ground, on p. 172 he says, "Peu s'en faut que je ne change d'opinion," two pages later he finally capitulates, and on p. 179 he says, "Je m'asseure que vous ne trouverés mauvais, si pour parvenir à l'asseurée preuve de la verité, j'ay fait de l'opiniastre en ce que j'estimois mensonge." This method will be followed in the second dialogue; at the

end of the first (pp. 179–80) the participants agree that Nicot and Aubert will debate the next day, Aubert maintaining that laws, honor,
and virtue are only opinion.

> RONSARD. C'estoit au commencement l'opinion de BAIF.
>
> AUBERT. Et puis qu'il l'a voulu, ce sera demain la mienne.

Aubert prepares to accept his role with enthusiasm: "J'ay deliberé de
faire l'opiniastre à toutes restes."

This is only part of the artificial air De Brués gives to his dialogue. Time is emphasized throughout: the dialogue begins about
mid-day and ends at sunset, and frequent references are made to the
passing of time. Baïf's view—"en tout n'y a qu'opinion"—runs
through the argument like a *leit-motiv* or the refrain of a ballad. The
argumentative techniques used are often transparently unfair or irrelevant: on p. 99 Baïf is talking about "les loix" and Ronsard about
"la loy," so that naturally they cannot agree. Baïf's point of view is
the most striking and the easiest to defend, but Ronsard is given the
more effective arguments. However, whenever Ronsard scores a point,
Baïf simply refuses to be convinced, or changes the subject, or launches
into down-to-earth analogies which cannot possibly apply to meta-
physics and serve simply to confuse the issue. On pp. 164–65 Ronsard
attempts the Socratic method of interrogation, but Baïf refuses to play:
"Je voy bien, tu me veux faire confesser par tes inductions, que je sçay
ce qu'auparavant je n'ay pas sceu: mais tu n'es pas encore là où tu
penses." On p. 177 there is a very curious and wholly artificial speech
by Baïf, an ecstatic outpouring of admiration for God and his works
which is in no way prepared for by the previous argument.

While the subject matter appears entirely serious, then, the general
tone of the dialogue is often playful, and the tension between these
two attitudes provides an excellent example of Renaissance bluff. Montaigne took a good deal from De Brués for the "Apologie de Raymond
Sebond," but De Brués's technique is closer to that of Rabelais. He
expounds philosophical doctrines in a literary, artificial, and often

playful context, whereas Rabelais expresses serious views on religion and other matters in a context of farce.

An interesting contrast to De Brués is provided by another dialogue writer who is practically unknown today, Jacques Tahureau.[32] His two *Dialogues du Democritic* (1565) are so odd, indeed, that I am not at all sure what to make of them. Did Tahureau intend to provoke exactly this reaction? If he did, we have here a very successful example of bluff.

The dialogues are preceded by an *epistre* by M. de La Porte, heavily emphasizing the moral content of the work. M. de La Porte was obviously particularly attracted by the antifeminism of the first dialogue, and he adds his own contribution on woman, "de toutes creatures la plus imparfaite" (p. vii). He summarizes the content of the dialogues briefly and clearly regards the whole work as a condemnation of human stupidity. The title confirms this impression: *Les dialogues de feu Jaques Tahureau gentilhomme du Mans, non moins profitables que facetieus, ou les vices d'un châcun sont repris fort âprement, pour nous animer davantage à les fuir et suivre la vertu.* And in his *advertissement* Tahureau claims that his purpose was to "bien dire et croire avecques un ou peu de gens de bon esprit . . . m'estant du tout appuié sur le fondement de la raison, et non point d'authorité humaine simplement forgée de quelque pauvre cerveau renversé" (p. xv). He then apologizes to the ladies for his pejorative opinions and rough language (of course, they will admit "qu'il y a je ne sçai quoi en l'homme plus grand et plus parfait qu'en la femme"), and ends with the statement of "mon intention, qui n'est encline à autre chose qu'à complaire aus honestes dames et à toutes autres personnes biennées, et n'aiant cet oeuvre entrepris à autre fin que pour adoucir le travail et recréer le loisir des hommes de sain et entier jugement" (p. xvi). *Castigat ridendo mores,* in fact, or the commonplace Renaissance combination of *l'utile* and *l'agréable,* and we expect a rather dull moral

---

[32] *Les dialogues de Jacques Tahureau gentilhomme du Mans,* ed. F. Conscience (Paris, 1870). Page references in the text are to this edition.

treatise on human foibles led by Le Democritic, the main character, whose name recalls the philosopher Democritus, who laughed at human folly (instead of weeping like Heraclitus).

After all this moralizing build-up the dialogues come as a considerable surprise. The first one certainly begins with a self-satisfied monologue by Le Democritic, condemning the lack of reason of his fellow men; when Le Cosmophile arrives, he asks humbly for moral instruction on "quelles choses sont à suyvre des hommes, et quelles à eviter" (p. 4). But most of the first dialogue is taken up with a violent denunciation of women and the Petrarchan love convention by Le Democritic, who at one point launches into a sixteen-page tirade on the subject. Moreover, in spite of his name, Le Democritic is not laughing but sneering and satirizing with bitter scorn and surprising violence for a *philosophe.* And there are other curious aspects of this antifeminist section. We tend to assume that the dominant personality in a dialogue is the mouthpiece of the author, and there is no doubt that Le Democritic is dominant—he flattens the weak-willed Cosmophile like a steam roller. But is his violent antifeminism to be attributed to Tahureau, whose other works consist of precious or sensual love poetry and who is reputed (by Colletet) to have died "of love" a few days after his marriage? [33] We cannot so conclude. A closer look at this section of the work shows that Le Democritic is not being quite the straightforward moralist he would like us to think. There is, after all, nothing fundamentally vicious about being in love. Le Cosmophile's attitude, that love is a refining and educating force, is attacked by Le Democritic not because it is vicious or morally wrong but because it is stupid. And it is stupid because it is artificial and has no rational basis.

What we have here, in fact, is a confrontation of two irreconcilable attitudes, both of which are essentially literary and not real. Le

---

[33] For an example of Tahureau's poetry, see Prosper Blanchemain, ed., *Mignardises amoureuses de l'admirée* (Geneva, 1868).

Cosmophile is a supporter of the tradition which leads from the troubadours via Petrarch and Castiglione to the feminist poets of the Renaissance—love is an ennobling and educating force, and women are to be respected and looked up to. Le Democritic represents the much older antifeminist tradition, nourished by theological and medical theories of woman's inferiority and abundantly illustrated in French literature from the *fabliaux* to the *Quinze joyes de mariage* and beyond. Moreover, the basic argument, as stated by Tahureau, reduces to a question of language. Le Cosmophile has been brought up on the elegant and refined language of works like Castiglione's *Book of the Courtier,* while Le Democritic speaks with the earthy and pungent directness of the farces and the *contes.* Their names may even have been chosen to emphasize the fact that they are talking on two quite different planes: *Le Democritic* suggests philosophy, and one would expect his interlocutor to be Heraclitus, whereas *Le Cosmophile,* "he who loves the world," is a pejorative formation of the kind Henri Estienne will use. The characters in his *Deux dialogues du langage françois italianisé* (1578) are Philausone, "the lover of Italy," Celthophile, "the lover of France," and Philalèthe, "the lover of truth." Le Democritic's main objection to courtly love is precisely that its language and gestures are artificial. He rails against the meaningless coquettish remarks of ladies to their admirers (pp. 23–26) and the affected gestures of courtiers (p. 33). His satire of lawyers and doctors is similarly based on the respect they acquire merely by their appearance, and he warns Le Cosmophile, "N'estime plus doresnavant qu'il y ait une si grande simpathie de l'exterieur avecques l'interieur que pour un marcher et gravité contrefaicte, pour un deguisement d'habits outre le vulgaire (folies communes en telle maniere de gens) le cerveau en soit plus meur et rassis, comme s'il y avoit quelque energie et occulte proprieté aux vestemens pour rendre l'esprit de l'homme pire ou meilleur" (p. 82).

So far from being a general moral treatise, then, the first dialogue is mainly anticourtier, and the "vices" held up for scorn are mainly artifi-cialities of language. Now Tahureau surely knows that the *esprit gaulois* tradition which Le Democritic upholds with such gusto is itself a literary convention. The only sensible explanation of this dialogue, to my mind, is that Tahureau is enjoying the clash between opposing attitudes, ex-pressed respectively in "style grave" and "style bas," as Ronsard might put it, and is also enjoying giving the upper hand to a point of view diametrically opposed to his own in other works.

The second dialogue is a little more general in scope, but here again most of it concentrates on one kind of folly—alchemy and as-trology. And here again Le Democritic's basic objection is linguistic: the main vice of alchemists is that "pour deguiser les matieres ils usent d'autres mots qu'on ne fait vulgairement" (p. 139), and soldiers are by no means "plus vaillans soubs l'ombre d'un je renie Dieu proferé de bonne grace, ou quand ils portent le bonnet haut eslevé par dessus le front" (p. 146). Le Democritic's tone is just as savage in this dia-logue. He condemns atheists and Mohammedans with the same vio-lent energy as women, and some of his condemnations are a little too sweeping to be taken seriously. Within a few pages, and on the flimsy pretext that one must not blindly follow authority, he demol-ishes Agrippa and Cardanus, Plato and Aristotle, Fregoso and Eras-mus. I cannot believe that Tahureau is serious here, especially since two pages earlier he has admitted that mockery "fardee et couverte de dissimulation" is excusable (p. 155).

There is nothing ambiguous about Le Democritic's point of view toward the follies he is condemning, but his attitude is often intrigu-ing, to say the least. In the course of the second dialogue Le Cosmo-phile points out to him that he really isn't at all like Democritus (p. 150) and asks him "la raison qui t'incite de faire ainsi du Prothée changeant tes parolles en tant de diverses manieres." Le Democritic replies that he adapts his tone to his public and that anyway Democ-ritus was very far from perfect. At Le Cosmophile's request he defines "le vraye maniere de se moquer": "Moquerie c'est le mépris non aucunement feint ni dissimulé d'une chose sote et ridicule, fait avecques raison et bonne grace" (p. 155).

Are these dialogues, then, intended as demonstrations of the art of mockery? But *bonne grace* is the last qualifier one would apply to some of Le Democritic's tirades against women and alchemists, and as we have seen, his mockery is often too savage to be called mockery at all. Le Cosmophile is occasionally playful—he says at one point, "Ce que je t'en avoi dit n'estoit seulement que pour sçavoir quel jugement tu en donnerais" (p. 22)—but Le Democritic's attitude throughout is deadly serious, though often expressed in language so strong and earthy that the reader finds it hard to take him seriously.

One is left wondering, in fact, just what the main point of this work is, and considering the possibility that Tahureau is playing with ambiguity. The book is a condemnation not of vice, as it claims, but of the dangerous discrepancy between external appearance or language and internal reality. Le Democritic says he is laughing and is, in fact, sneering; says he uses *raison* and, in fact, overreacts violently to quite venial defects; emphasizes *bonne grace* and is, in fact, usually graceless and tasteless. His views on medicine, astrology, and atheists could well be Tahureau's own, while those on love and women surely could not. It is this ambiguity which makes the work still entertaining to read, and unless Tahureau was an improbably insensitive man, the ambiguity must be intentional.

To take a final example of bluff from the dialogue genre, the most striking sixteenth-century victim of the either/or complex is Bonaventure Des Périers. His (if it is his) [34] *Cymbalum mundi* runs to forty-three pages in the most recent edition,[35] and a complete bibliography on it would occupy about the same space.[36] Did forty-three

---

[34] Professor Screech remains unconvinced; see "The Meaning of the Title *Cymbalum mundi*," *BHR* XXXI (1969), 343–45. If the work is not by Des Périers, then the theories of Saulnier and Nurse about its meaning fall to the ground, since they are largely based on his other works.

[35] By Peter H. Nurse, 2nd ed. (Manchester: Manchester University Press, 1967).

[36] Such bibliographies are available; see V.-L. Saulnier, "Le sens du *Cymbalum mundi* de Bonaventure Des Périers," *BHR* XIII (1951), 43–69, 137–71; and D. Neidhart,

pages ever provoke such controversy? Among other ingenious interpretations, the author has been proved, by the most diverse analytical methods, to be a militant rationalist, an opponent of Calvin's *Institutes,* a Cabalistic symbolist, a straightforward imitator of Lucian, a *hésuchiste,* and a *libertin spirituel*.[37] These critical arguments and counterarguments have been entertaining readers for some fifty years and, I suspect, would have greatly entertained the author, but it does not seem to have occurred to anyone that Des Périers may have deliberately cast his dialogues in an ambiguous form.

After all, if he did write them in order to uphold or demolish a particular point of view, the attempt was clearly a failure. The only obvious thing about them is their disconcerting aspect. The four dialogues have a certain amount of continuity of theme and character but no true continuity, so that each has to be considered separately. Some anagrams are obvious (Tryocan, Rhetulus, Cubercus), while some are completely mysterious (Byrphanes, Ardelio, and I am by no means convinced that Drarig is Erasmus). The character of Mercury has a long literary and polemical history and notoriously lends itself to opposing interpretations. There is considerable use, as in Rabelais, of ambiguous themes like wine and speech. The allegory of some episodes is obvious: the second dialogue must be satirizing theologians who all claim true knowledge of the Word of God. But in other episodes contradictory interpretations come at once to mind: Jupiter's book of destiny could be a reference to the contemporary craze for prognostications and prophecies or to the theological arguments about predestination.

The much-discussed final dialogue between the two dogs Pamphagus and Hylactor—names of which almost any interpretation can be, and has been, given—is full of intriguing ambiguities. In the last three pages of the Nurse edition we find (1) a discussion on the

---

Das Cymbalum mundi des Bonaventure Des Périers, Forschungslage und Deutung (Geneva: Droz; Paris: Minard, 1959).

[37] By, respectively, the majority of critics, including Lefranc, Busson, and Febvre; Walser; Just; Mayer; Saulnier; and Nurse.

foolish curiosity of men and their constant desire for something new—one of the main satirical points of the whole work, according to Saulnier; (2) Pamphagus's conclusion that silence is more effective than speech; (3) Pamphagus's remark, "Car tu ne boys point de vin, comme je croy," which could be a simple statement of fact—dogs do not drink wine—or a reference to the Eucharist; (4) a mysterious reference to a packet of letters addressed to "Messieurs les Antipodes"; (5) Hylactor's list of fables, most of which concern miracles or transformations and one of which ("Erus qui revesquit") could be a reference to Christ. All five points have provoked critical argument and widely differing interpretations; can it be a coincidence that this little work is so packed with ambiguity? I think it very likely that it is not a coincidence and that Des Périers is deliberately exploiting what he knows to be the taste of his contemporaries. A dangerous game, of course, and until very recently he was condemned or praised as an out-and-out rationalist, one of the most unfair judgments in the whole of literary history.

Here we have some very diverse examples of Renaissance bluff in action. Marguerite de Navarre uses argument to present opposing points of view which are never reconciled, and the interest is apparently in the argument itself rather than in the conclusion. De Brués goes much further and transforms a polemical philosophical argument into a work of art by playing with *vraisemblance* techniques, fair and unfair arguments, and the whole concept of seriousness. Of these four writers, he is the one who is most obviously using bluff, but if I am right about Tahureau and Des Périers, they are doing the same thing, only much more subtly. Tahureau's dialogues actually condemn very different things from what they claim, and the *Cymbalum mundi* is at the same time an entertaining work of fiction and an exercise in ambiguity. None of these authors uses all the bluff techniques I have enumerated, but each of them uses one or two in a conscious effort to disconcert the reader.

I am not attempting here to classify these techniques or to assess

which of them is most often used by Renaissance authors. Whole
books have been written on ambiguity, irony, and paradox, and I
have no startling new theory to add to the existing analyses of them.
My main concern in this book is the effect produced by bluff techniques in the works of Rabelais and Montaigne, and this effect is
so complex, compounded of so many different elements, that to
sort out irony from paradox or enigma from ambiguity would be impossible. Even if possible, it would not necessarily be relevant; what
I am concentrating on is not the point of departure in the mind of
the author but the overall effect of the text as perceived by the reader.
What the author intended to do can never be fully known, but what
he did do is there on the page, a fair battleground for all.

This brief analysis of a few contemporary authors was intended
to show that Rabelais and Montaigne were not isolated eccentrics
writing in a void. The subjects which preoccupied them, and the style
they used, are those of their time. There is no doubt that they did
what they were doing a great deal better than any of their contemporaries, but it is essential to recognize that they did the same
kind of thing as the authors just discussed.

Before we go on to a detailed study of Rabelais and Montaigne, a
few more words of warning are perhaps in order. I have already
pointed out that when discussing ambiguity, we must make quite
sure that the ambiguity is present in the text and is not simply a
result of our lack of knowledge of the period, the writer, or the subject. Similarly, we must be careful to distinguish paradox from bathos
and true paradox from false. In a true paradox there is an intellectual
opposition between two elements, whereas in bathos the elements
are simply juxtaposed. Both techniques produce a comic effect, but
only paradox will provoke reflection or put its own nature in question.[38] While the Renaissance delights in true paradoxes, it sometimes
plays with false ones as though they were true. One of these is

[38] These problems are sensibly discussed in the introduction to Colie's *Paradoxia
Epidemica* (see note 7).

utile/doux, a rhetorical opposition which does not reflect a genuine problem. Most important, we must firmly renounce a modern dichotomy which simply does not apply to the Renaissance—the opposition between comic and serious. Like the similarly artificial one between *forme* and *fond,* it will not stand up to a detailed examination. We have already seen De Brués being simultaneously serious and playful, and this coexistence is precisely Rabelais's enduring genius.

Armed with these warnings, let us examine the works of Rabelais and Montaigne to see if they bear out my contention that theirs was the age of bluff.

Rabelais and
the Techniques of Shock

Rabelais, like the authors discussed in the previous chapter, grew up in an atmosphere favorable to the expression of paradox, ambiguity, and the other bluff techniques already enumerated. One suspects also that something in his temperament must have inclined him in this direction, for his book stands out, even in the paradoxical climate of his age, as one of the most disconcerting works of fiction ever penned. What I hope to show in this chapter is that Rabelais's main aim is to shock, startle, or disconcert his reader. He does this by using a multiplicity of bluff techniques which I shall not attempt to classify in order of importance. To treat them in any general way, with il-lustrations from each book, would be confusing and repetitive, and it seems both clearer and more logical to deal with the four books in the order in which they were written. I have deliberately omitted all discussion of the fifth book, although I suspect that parts of it are by Rabelais. Most modern critics, from Lefebvre to Paris, assume that the book is authentic because it agrees with their theories; this is not to my mind a justifiable procedure. In the present state of lack of evidence about the book I can only say that I wish Rabelais had written at least some of it, particularly the final chapters, but since I do not know that he did, I cannot take it into account here.

The chronological order I have adopted has its disadvantages but is, I think, to be preferred for two reasons. First, I wish to concentrate attention on how these books must have appeared to a contemporary reader; second, Rabelais's preoccupation with bluff techniques changed emphasis considerably as successive books were written. What began as an intellectual game became a profound interest in the very nature of ambiguity and our reactions to it, and the order in which the books were written is, therefore, of major importance.

To emphasize Rabelais's delight in ambiguity and paradox is by no means to deny his serious purposes. Of course he is instructing his reader (on education, religion, navigation, dress-making, or whatever it may be) while amusing him, of course many of his grievances are deeply felt, and of course Professor Screech is right in his painstaking approach to Rabelais's text. I would support nearly all of Screech's interpretations; indeed, my enormous debt to him will be abundantly obvious throughout this chapter. Although I find many new critical approaches, especially those of Michel Butor and Jean Paris, interesting and stimulating, I remain suspicious of them because they are often not based on a sound knowledge of what the text means in sixteenth-century terms. My own emphasis on bluff is intended not to distort the text in any overly modern way but to help redress the imbalance created by a generation of critics, from Lefranc to Telle, who have overemphasized the "serious" content at the expense of the humor.

BOOK ONE

Let us first examine *Pantagruel,* then, with an eye on that 1532 reader with whom we cannot completely identify, but whom we must endeavor to understand as far as possible. What is he expecting when he picks up the book in the bookshop and begins leafing through it?

Judging by the title (*Les horribles et espoventables faictz et prouesses du tresrenommé Pantagruel Roy des Dipsodes, filz du grand geant Gargantua*) and a cursory glance through the prologue, he will expect another facetious adventure story, like the *Grandes et inestimables cronicques du grant et enorme geant Gargantua* or the *Grande et merveilleuse vie du trespuissant et redoubté Roy Gargantua,* a parody of the epic with only one basic comic technique: the disparity in size between a giant and his friends or enemies.[1] If our reader is a humanist, he may be alerted by three aspects of the prologue: the references to evangelical matters, the style (vastly superior already to that of the genre in general), and the first sentence: "Tres illustres et tres chevalereux champions, gentilz hommes *et aultres.* . . ."[2] If he is a gentleman farmer or a printer's apprentice, he will probably not notice any of these things.

He buys the book, then, takes it home, and begins to read it. If he is a "general reader," he will enjoy chapters 1–7 without trouble, since if there is more erudition than he had bargained for, it is obviously comic and so he won't bother his head about it. But the humanist, accustomed to looking closely at style, will immediately notice a masterly use of such comic linguistic devices as disproportionate comparison: Hurtaly sits astride the ark like a child on a wooden horse or a soldier on a cannon. If he has waited to buy the 1533 edition, he will also find some typically Rabelaisian use of bathos: "Qui engendra Fierabras, lequel fut vaincu par Olivier, pair de France, compaignon de Roland, Qui engendra Morguan, lequel premier de ce monde joua aux dez avecques ses bezicles." By the second chapter he will have a good idea of the kind of style he is dealing with: vivid, breathless, using a constant shift in context and tone to give a

---

[1] These and other contemporary chapbooks are discussed by Marcel Françon in his edition of *Le vroy Gargantua* (Paris: Nizet, 1949).

[2] My italics. References for the first three books are to the critical edition begun by Abel Lefranc and others and still in progress: vols. I and II (*Gargantua*) in 1913, vols. III and IV (*Pantagruel*) in 1922, and vol. V (*Tiers livre*) in 1931 (Paris: Champion). As only one volume of the *Quart livre* has appeared (Geneva: Droz, 1955), my references from the *Quart livre* are to the Jourda edition (Paris: Garnier, 1962).

surprise effect. In this sentence, for instance—"Vous les [les hommes] eussiez veuz tirans la langue, comme levriers qui ont couru six heures; plusieurs se gettoyent dedans les puys; aultres se mettoyent au ventre d'une vache pour estre à l'hombre, et les appelle Homere *Alibantes*"— he will find several techniques typical of Rabelais. First, the vivid comparisons, based on action rather than description and reinforced by numerical precision; second, the shift from men to greyhounds and back to men; and chiefly, the surprise ending to the sentence. Homer is not only irrelevant to the context, since one does not expect Classical erudition in a folktale, he is also anachronistic here, and the anachronism is neatly pointed up by the present tense (*appelle*).

Our humanist may decide at this point, as a similarly educated reader would today, to analyze in more detail a longer Rabelaisian sentence. I have chosen a very long and quite complex one, typical of Rabelais's manner in the first book and to some extent in the second, but much less frequent in the later books:

> Le Philosophe raconte, en mouvent la question pour quoy c'est que l'eaue de la mer est salée, que, au temps que Phebus bailla le gouvernement de son chariot lucificque à son filz Phaeton, ledict Phaeton, mal apris en l'art et ne sçavant ensuyvre la line ecliptique entre les deux tropiques de la sphere du soleil, varia de son chemin et tant approcha de terre qu'il mist à sec toutes les contrées subjacentes, bruslant une grande partie du ciel que les Philosophes appellent *Via lactea* et les lifrelofres nomment *le chemin Sainct Jacques,* combien que les plus huppez poetes disent estre la part où tomba le laict de Juno lors qu'elle allaicta Hercules: adonc la terre fut tant eschaufée que il luy vint une sueur enorme, dont elle sua toute la mer, qui par ce est salée, car toute sueur est salée; ce que vous direz estre vray si vous voulez taster de la vostre propre, ou bien de celles des verollez quand on les faict suer; ce me est tout un.

The well-educated and sensitive reader, then or now, will notice in particular the following points; they are not intended to be conclusive or exclusive, but they are all related to paradox or ambiguity.

1) The whole sentence is a magnificent irrelevance, having nothing to do with Pantagruel's birth and very little connection with the thirsty countryside Rabelais has just been describing. It is a good example of his chatty and digressive style and of his habit of exhausting all the possible aspects of a subject, whether relevant or not, before passing on to the next one.

2) *Le Philosophe raconte* looks like false erudition, adduced to give credence to a fanciful statement; the erudition is, however, quite genuine. The philosopher is Empedocles, and even if the contemporary reader does not know Plutarch's *De placitis philosophorum,* he will be familiar with the story of Phaeton from Ovid's *Metamorphoses.*

3) *au temps que* looks like the beginning of a "once upon a time when" clause but turns out immediately to mean simply "when."

4) *lucificque* is a learned adjective, probably composed by Rabelais, and is in comic contradiction to the more colloquial *bailler.*

5) The technical terminology (*ecliptique* and *tropiques*) is not relevant in the context and is another anachronism.

6) The clause beginning *bruslant une grande partie du ciel* has no connection with the previous clause, which concerned the earth.

7) *Philosophes,* accompanied by *Via lactea,* forms a comic contrast to *lifrelofres* and *chemin Sainct Jacques,* but the similarity of sound between *Philosophes* and *lifrelofres* makes one suspect that Rabelais is in fact assimilating, not contrasting, them.

8) The concessive clause beginning *combien que* already suggests a doubt about the validity of what follows, and this doubt is reinforced both by the adjective *huppez* and by the fact that this is a contention made by poets (not philosophers). The mythological explanation of natural phenomena was, of course, already suspect in Classical times; in any case, it is an irrelevant elaboration here, since the Milky Way has nothing to do with the subjects of this chapter.

9) By the time we get to *Hercules,* the whole sentence appears to

be bogging down. We have had seven dependent clauses after the main verb, so that although the conjunctions are logical, there are too many of them for comfort. Instead of stopping the sentence here, Rabelais merely pauses for breath and then starts off again with a firm *adonc,* which sums up the whole of the previous development from *au temps que.*

10) The five clauses following *adonc* seem to constitute a scientific explanation, but this impression is contradicted by their construction, which is not smooth and looks haphazard rather than logical. It is typical of Rabelais, in all four books, to keep adding to a sentence when we think we have come to the end of it.

11) The next section (*ce que . . . la vostre propre*) looks like a plea for experimental science and the verification of hypotheses by personal experience. This impression is at once contradicted by the following revolting suggestion, presented on the same plane and with the same syntax as the previous one.

12) The final clause is very short, monosyllabic, and direct, in complete contrast to the rest of this rambling, digressive sentence. It is also delightfully detached in tone, but this detachment, as well as referring to what immediately precedes, could include the subject matter of the whole sentence. In this case, if Rabelais really doesn't mind one way or the other, why has he just expended so much energy and enthusiasm? This, too, is typical, as we shall see; one of Rabelais's major comic devices is the lavish expenditure of energy on trivial pretexts.

This type of analysis could be applied to many of the sentences in *Pantagruel,* but the one quoted here is an excellent illustration of the types of bluff Rabelais uses on the linguistic level. The careful reader is constantly disconcerted because he is constantly changing gear to cope with Rabelais's shifts in syntax, vocabulary, context, and tone.

Let us move on now to consider our humanist's reflections after he has finished the book. I do not need to stress the pleasure he will have gotten from the verbal comedy, which has been discussed in detail by many critics.[3] But he will have noticed increasingly how this comedy is applied to situations not in themselves comic. Gargantua's dilemma in chapter 3—should he weep for the death of his wife or rejoice at the birth of his son—is of the same type as many a philosophical problem, and his mixture of colloquial, pathetic, and Platonic language increases the comedy but does not detract from the "serious" implications. Episodes like that of the *écolier limousin* and the meeting with Panurge (the importance of language as a means of communication), the Baisecul-Humevesne lawsuit (the irrelevance of legal language to its subject matter), the discussion by signs with Thaumaste (to what extent can one resolve philosophical doubts?), Panurge's skirmishes with the lady (the unnaturalness of courtly love conventions), and the author's adventures in Pantagruel's mouth (the relativity of our ideas about "our" world) are similarly susceptible of interpretation on different levels.

But we should not assume that the "serious" aspect of an episode will be straightforwardly satirical. In the case of Panurge and his lady it is, but the other episodes just mentioned are more complicated. The speeches by the two litigants, and Pantagruel's judgment, are developments of the *coq-à-l'âne,* very popular in the theater and poetry at this time. The whole point of the *coq-à-l'âne* is its suspense value —you keep thinking that something intelligible is coming through. Is Rabelais comparing this technique to the incomprehensible jargon of lawyers, or is he satirizing them by using a different kind of incomprehensibility from theirs? The Thaumaste episode is more complex yet. Chapter 18 is a subtle mixture of comedy and what seems to be a genuine desire for knowledge.[4] Thaumaste introduces himself as

[3] Especially by Marcel Tetel, *Etude sur le comique de Rabelais,* Biblioteca dell' *Archivum Romanicum,* ser. I, vol. LXIX (Florence: L. S. Olschki, 1964). Unfortunately, the author treats Rabelais's comedy as the only valid and interesting aspect of his work, deliberately ignoring the "serious" content.

[4] These chapter numbers are from the 1541 edition used by Lefranc; the 1532 arrangement of chapters can be found in V.-L. Saulnier's *Pantagruel, édition critique sur le texte original,* T.L.F. (Paris: Droz, 1946).

an unsatisfied seeker after truth, but his enumeration of other truth-seekers who have acted in the same way goes on too long, tending to create the portrait of just another pedant. His reason for proposing a debate in sign language is delightfully ambiguous: "Car les matieres sont tant ardues que les parolles humaines ne seroyent suffisantes à les expliquer à mon plaisir." This looks like satire; however unsatisfactory words may be, they are surely a better means of communication than the deaf-and-dumb language. But in view of Rabelais's attacks on the misuse and abuse of language, he may mean that signs, at least, are not ambiguous and may be more helpful.

Pantagruel's graceful and elegantly phrased reply suggests that he is taking all this seriously, but his attitude is in comic contrast to the insouciance of Panurge, and the use of Panurge rather than Pantagruel to combat Thaumaste would also suggest that the discussion is mainly facetious. There are, moreover, several references in this chapter to the themes of size and thirst, which in this book are almost always the mainspring of purely facetious episodes.

The next chapter provides an excellent example of Rabelaisian bluff of this period. First of all, the detailed description of the signs formed is comic by its length, minuteness, and sheer ingenuity and provokes a roar of laughter the moment we realize that the signs are nearly all rude gestures. Then, after each disputant has made only one series of gestures, Thaumaste, forgetting that he must not speak, suddenly says, "Et si Mercure. . . ." It is very difficult to say in what order our reactions occur at this point, but I would suggest that something like the following takes place. First we laugh because the rule of silence is broken. Then we reflect how intensely absorbed in the discussion Thaumaste must be to forget himself like this. And then we begin to wonder how Mercury could possibly be relevant to the philosophical debate in progress. It is remotely within the bounds of possibility that he might be—Mercury, as well as the messenger of the gods, is the patron of alchemy, which is one of the subjects Thaumaste had trouble with. But it is difficult to imagine Mercury represented by sign language at all, more difficult to imagine a discussion including such a specific conditional or concessive clause portrayed in sign language, and quite impossible that the discussion could have got to this point so soon. All these elements are, I think, present in our laughter at this point, and the slight doubt over the relevance of Mercury constitutes the "bluff" element.[5]

When the debate concludes in the following chapter, we are left wondering who the dupe really is. Is Panurge making fun of a genuine, if not overbright, searcher after knowledge? Is Thaumaste a fool to have suggested using sign language? Oh is he not rather a fool because he hoped to resolve his *problemes insolubles* by this method? Either a problem can be resolved or it cannot, and if it cannot, why should sign language be more help than speech? The answer many critics would give to these questions is that Rabelais is simply enjoying himself by exercising verbal ingenuity, but it seems far more likely that he has deliberately presented this episode in such a way as to make us question our established ideas on communication and to leave us groping in a mental fog. Of course, the whole thing is also a satire of scholastic debates, but very superficially, since Rabelais knew perfectly well that the scholastic debate was never intended to resolve philosophical and metaphysical problems like Thaumaste's, whether soluble or not.[6] One might say, as of the sentence analyzed above, that the conclusion negates the entire proceeding, since *prob-*

---

[5] My colleague, Professor John J. Bateman, points out that Mercury, among his many other functions, is known as the god of speech (cf. W. S. Roscher, *Ausführliches Lexikon der griechischen und römischen Mythologie* (Leipzig, 1894–97), II.2, 2822. The reference is to Martianus Capella, *De nuptiis Philologiae et Mercurii*). To invoke the god of speech in the middle of a debate in sign language is obviously an excellent joke.

[6] It has recently been convincingly suggested that the major import of this episode is political; see Ruth Murphy, "Rabelais, Thaumaste and the King's Great Matter," in *Studies in French Literature Presented to H. W. Lawton* (Manchester: Manchester University Press, 1968), pp. 261–85. This interpretation need not invalidate mine or the still more sweeping one of Jean Paris, *Rabelais au futur* (Paris: Seuil, 1970), p. 93: "Cette conteste de Thaumaste et de Panurge se propose en parabole de l'oeuvre entière."

lemes insolubles are clearly not worth debating. So Rabelais will construct the entire *Tiers livre* as an answer to an inquiry of Panurge's which is obviously a silly question and not worth answering at all.

I should like to discuss many other episodes from this point of view, but this one can stand as a good example. Let us now consider the book as a whole, still bearing in mind our sixteenth-century reader who was expecting a funny adventure story about giants. Is this what he got? Of a total of thirty-four chapters, only seven (2, 4, 5, 28, 29, 32, and 33) are mainly concerned with size and its comic potential, though references to size are scattered through the other chapters. This is startling enough, but what is more surprising still is that only fifteen chapters, less than half the total, are mainly concerned with action (2, 4, 5, 14, 16, 17, parts of 21, 22, 25, 26, 28, 29, 31, 32, and 33). That is to say that twenty chapters (1, 3, 6, 7, 8, 9, 10, 11, 12, 13, 15, 18, 19, 20, parts of 21, 23, 24, 27, 30, and 34) are based on intellectual and linguistic devices or deal with matters which are not funny at all. Moreover, an astonishing total of eight chapters (6, 7, 9, 11, 12, 13, 19, and 24) gain their comic effect from enigma or incomprehensibility. Our gentleman farmer and our printer's apprentice must be very puzzled, if not annoyed, by all this, but our humanist will, of course, be delighted. What could be a better joke than to enclose satire, paradox, and evangelism in the worn framework of a popular tale? The *grandes chroniques* were a parody of the epic, so Rabelais has provided a parody of a parody.

This is only the most obvious of the contradictory aspects of *Pantagruel.* There is also a constant shift of atmosphere, from chapter to chapter and within chapters, whose main purpose appears to be to disconcert the reader. Chapter 1 reads like a parody of the epic, chapter 29 like a genuine epic, the second half of chapter 24 like something out of a Persian fairy tale, and chapter 8 like a humanist manifesto. If it is serious, chapter 8 is the only completely noncomic chapter in the book and is certainly the first chapter which is not obviously facetious.[7] It is preceded by the magnificent learned satire of the library of St. Victor and followed by the very funny meeting with Panurge. It is possible that the letter is a parody of a style, so well done that it has been taken as serious, but in any case the shock effect created by its difference from the surrounding chapters is considerable.

There are fewer obviously "serious" passages in *Pantagruel* than in the other books, and with the exception of Gargantua's letter they all occur in otherwise facetious chapters. The passages with an evangelical ring are well camouflaged in the mixture of mock epic and mock folklore which dominates the war with the Dipsodes. In chapter 28 Pantagruel gives some typically evangelical advice to his prisoner, just after handing him a box of drugs which will terminate the war in what one might think a rather unsporting way. In chapter 29 occurs the much-debated prayer, followed immediately by the comic death of Loup-Garou. Specialists in Reformation problems have demonstrated that this prayer makes reference to several cruxes of debate between Lutherans and non-Lutherans, and that Rabelais is firmly stating an Erasmian position.[8] It is possible, of course, that he is no more "sincere" here than elsewhere and that he simply finds an evangelical style an excellent shock contrast to a mock fairy-tale one. I think that the prayer is genuine, if only because the best possible contrast to the facetious atmosphere of the adjacent passages is, precisely, authenticity. But Rabelais's inner motives, which we are never likely to know completely, do not affect the contrast in styles.

There are more subtle shifts in atmosphere, from chapter to chapter and within chapters, than the obvious shifts from seriousness to comedy. Chapters 4 and 5 are comedy of action, chapters 6 and 7 comedy of language. This is important; in the first and second books comedy of action and language are separate (though there are indi-

[7] In an entertaining article, " 'Ung abysme de science': On the Interpretation of Gargantua's Letter to Pantagruel," *BHR* XXVIII (1966), 615–32, G. J. Brault attempts to prove that the letter was never intended to be taken seriously. His arguments are not altogether convincing.

[8] See, most recently, M. A. Screech, *L'évangélisme de Rabelais*, T.H.R., vol. XXXII; *Etudes Rabelaisiennes*, vol. II (Geneva: Droz, 1959).

cations, as in *Pantagruel,* chs. 11–13, that they can be assimilated), whereas the *Tiers livre* will use language as action. Chapter 23 begins seriously with news of the death of Gargantua and the war with the Dipsodes, continues facetiously with the anecdote explaining why leagues are of different length in different countries, and ends with an enigma. Chapter 30 begins with grief over the death of Epistemon and goes on to a burlesque resurrection and a comic picture of life in the Underworld. Rabelais deliberately upset his conclusion to the book (ch. 34) by adding to the later editions a condemnation of monks which has no connection with the recital of Pantagruel's future fantastic exploits.

To return for a moment to the serious/comic dichotomy which modern critics apparently hope to find in Rabelais, there are indications that Rabelais started out in *Pantagruel* with a clear division in mind and that in the later books he deliberately blurred these clear outlines. In *Pantagruel* it seems obvious that we have serious issues presented comically (legal injustice in ch. 10), comic issues presented seriously (how to build the walls of Paris in ch. 15), as well as serious issues presented seriously (Gargantua's letter and Pantagruel's prayer), and, obviously, comic issues presented comically. In cases where we are not sure whose side the author is on, as in the Thaumaste debate already discussed, the basic problem is not of serious moral import.

In other words, the bluff process in *Pantagruel* is on the whole quite straightforward. There are plenty of shock tactics but little ambiguity, and the ambiguity is mainly on the parlor-game level. The chapters devoted to enigma show this very clearly. The *écolier limousin*'s speech in chapter 6 would present no difficulties for a humanist—he would find it funny but quite comprehensible, like the list of imaginary books in chapter 7, which is so painful for a modern reader. The assorted real and imaginary languages in chapter 9 do not need to be understood, although they are more comic if understood, because they are all saying the same thing, like the jargons in the famous scene from *Pathelin* which Rabelais is probably imitating. The lawsuit between Baisecul and Humevesne (chs. 11–13) is an extended exercise in *coq-à-l'âne* and is intended for immediate enjoyment rather than deciphering. The debate in sign language (ch. 19) is the most subtle example of enigma, for reasons already discussed. In chapter 24 we are back with the parlor game, which, on the pretext of deciphering an enigma, actually provides a display of erudition. Rabelais will make great use of this procedure in the *Tiers livre*.

The first part of this chapter is also an excellent example of a procedure already mentioned: the exuberant expenditure of energy on a pretext which is trivial, futile, or nonexistent. It may be that this is the basis of Rabelais's comic outlook; I have already noted a sentence whose ending negates the rest of it, and the energetically described gestures which cannot by definition solve Thaumaste's insoluble problems. Chapter 24 is a different kind of example, conceivably an allegory about scriptural interpretation. Panurge tries out every possible means of decipherment on the paper, only to discover that the key to the enigma was in the ring and consisted of two words from the New Testament. He has expended all his energy, and that of the Classical and imaginary authors he cites, to no purpose whatever.

This is, in fact, typical of Panurge. We first see him uselessly spouting strange tongues when he knows perfectly well that he has only to make his request in French and it will at once be gratified. Several chapters describe his tricks and sharp practices, all of which seem to entail more trouble than the result is worth. And his revenge on the lady, who has, after all, merely exercised her prerogative in saying "no," is fantastically elaborate. Through all his changes of character Panurge will retain this attribute—it is he who eulogizes debts and debtors for two chapters in the *Tiers livre,* and whose ridiculously garrulous fear in the face of danger animates a good deal of the *Quart livre.* It is this in particular which distinguishes him from Frere Jean, sometimes unfairly called his double. Frere Jean is also energetic and exuberant, but his energies are always directed to some precise and reasonable end—saving the vineyard, consoling Panurge on cuckoldry (*T.l.*, ch. 28), fighting the storm (*Q.l.*, chs. 18–24) or the hypocrites of Ganabin (*Q.l.*, ch. 66). Again, in the first book this procedure is not ambiguous, but I have mentioned it here at some length because it will become more ambiguous, and more important, later on.

I am unable to agree with Professor Screech that *Pantagruel* is a comparatively dull book.[9] On the contrary, I would say that there is never a dull moment; every chapter brings a new target under attack, displays new knowledge or a new interest, takes up the story in chronological order but on a different plane or in different language. The processes used to disconcert are on the whole straightforward, obvious, and always immensely entertaining. There seems to be no overriding moral purpose, such as one suspects in the later books, but rather a series of targets are set up, demolished, and then forgotten. It is the book of a man who has realized the comic and educational force of paradox and ambiguity but has not yet tried to explore their possibilities systematically.

BOOK TWO

It is clear from the title page onward that *La vie très horrificque du grand Gargantua père de Pantagruel. Jadis composée par M. Alcofribas, Abstracteur de Quinte Essence. Livre plein de Pantagruelisme* will always have one eye on its predecessor. If Rabelais's first book was a continuation of a popular legend, his second is, so to speak, a regression of his first. Regarding subject matter, he is rewriting the popular tale, which would seem to negate the very existence of his first book, since the biography of the father normally precedes that of the son (except in the medieval epic, where the story of the hero's father is

---

[9] See M. A. Screech, "Aspects of Rabelais' Christian Comedy," inaugural lecture delivered at London University, 2 Feb. 1967.

often written later. *Aimeri de Narbonne,* for instance, is the story of
the father of Guillaume d'Orange). At the same time Rabelais sets out
to write the same book all over again, since *Gargantua,* like *Pantagruel,*
consists of the same basic divisions: childhood, growing up through
education, maturity through war. And if the *Jadis* of the title looks
like a feeble attempt to explain away *Gargantua* as having been written first, he must have been well aware that no one was likely to be
deceived by it.

So the subject of the second book is already a sort of *pari*—he could,
after all, have written about Pantagruel's son and thereby had Panurge
meet Frere Jean with more *vraisemblance.* Can he, in fact, write the
same book all over again, using parallel characters (one giant father
and mother, one giant baby, one comic devoted companion, and several
serious ones), and get away with it? He can, of course, mainly by
varying the tone to such an extent that we forget the similarity of subject matter. As I have said elsewhere, whereas *Pantagruel* is destructive, tilting at any windmills which happen along, *Gargantua* is constructive. It shows us not only what must be destroyed but also what
must be built in its place. The book is full of solid objects—clothes,
books, bells, *fouaces,* citadels, cannonballs, and an abbey—which replace
the evanescent linguistic peculiarities on which *Pantagruel* is based.
People, too, have a more solid reality, and the giant world is much
closer to our world in spite of the many jokes based on size. One cannot imagine Gargantua delivering Pantagruel's summing-up of the
Baisecul-Humevesne lawsuit.

Let us look now at *Gargantua,* then, still bearing in mind the reactions of our sixteenth-century humanist, who is probably expecting
the same sort of book as *Pantagruel.* It has not been sufficiently emphasized by critics that the famous prologue to *Gargantua* is the prologue to the second book and that it indicates different preoccupations
from the prologue to the first.[10] In particular, it shows an interest and

10 There are interesting discussions of the prologues, with sharply differing points
of view, in Floyd Gray, "Ambiguity and Point of View in the Prologue to *Gargantua,*"

delight in double bluff, as opposed to the more direct bluff characteristic of *Pantagruel*. Rabelais begins, "Beuveurs tres illustres, et vous, Verolez tres precieux,—car à vous, non à aultres, sont dediez mes escriptz . . . ," and proceeds immediately to comment on a passage from Plato's *Symposium*. This might be a straightforward joke—*Beuveurs* and *Verolez* being unlikely to have read or enjoyed Plato—or it might, on the contrary, make the reader give a more subtle meaning to these two nouns. This is the first use by Rabelais of ambiguous themes, which will become an important feature of the next three books. These themes are wine, reproduction, illness, and madness, and each of them is susceptible not just of two interpretations, which would constitute direct bluff, but of more than two, which gives us double bluff. The reader of this prologue in 1534 cannot be aware of this, but he must be aware almost at once that paradox is the mainspring of the prologue.

The comparison of Socrates to a Silenus was a commonplace in the Renaissance. Rabelais livens it up by introducing the *Beuveurs* (and attaching them to the Silenus via Bacchus) and the *Verolez,* who did not exist in Socrates' day, by particularizing the description of the box and its contents and by exaggerating the description of Socrates (who was not, for example, "inepte à tous offices de la republique"). He then proceeds to compare his book to the contents of a Silenus, and the title to the exterior, which gives us a triple analogy: Silenus/Socrates/book, suggesting that as Socrates = Silenus and as book = Silenus, then book = Socrates. Before we conclude that the contents of *Gargantua* have the wisdom of Socrates, we should remember the war waged by the humanists on syllogistic reasoning.[11] Such an analogy in the fifteenth century might have been genuine; made by Rabelais, it is almost certainly a joke.

RR LVI (1965), 12–21; Dorothy Coleman, "The Prologues of Rabelais," *MLR* LXII (1967), 407–19; and Paris, *Rabelais au futur.*

[11] See, for example, Pontus de Tyard, *Le second curieux,* in *The Universe of Pontus de Tyard: A Critical Edition of L'univers,* ed. John C. Lapp (Ithaca, N.Y.: Cornell University Press, 1950), pp. 151–65.

The piling up of analogy is not finished. He next compares the reader to a man opening a bottle (of wine presumably; the *beuveur* theme again) and to a dog cracking a bone to get at the marrow. So we now have the analogy Silenus/Socrates/book/wine/marrow, which by its very proliferation is beginning to look less and less serious. He then states firmly that his book contains a "sustantificque mouelle"[12] of religious, moral, and ethical doctrine, but deliberately spoils the lofty tone of this declaration by qualifying *mysteres* with the adjective *horrificques*.

He goes on, in any case, to contradict himself completely by comparing his book to Classical works in which critics have found far more symbolic content than the author intended, and by putting himself among the wine-drinking poets who relied on their inspiration, as opposed to the oil-burning poets who preferred hard work and conscious effort. Wine has already acquired a broader significance than the first word of the prologue suggested, although Rabelais ends on a note similar to the beginning: "Vous soubvienne de boyre à my pour la pareille, et je vous plegeray tout ares metys."

A great deal of ink has been expended by oil-burning critics over the question of the dog, the bone, and the marrow. Is there a *sustantificque mouelle* or isn't there? To my mind the question is badly phrased. There are quite a few serious passages in *Gargantua*—more than there were in *Pantagruel*—but they are accessible without any bone-cracking. Rabelais's loves and hates are stated plainly, not hidden away in subtleties. The main interest of the prologue is its statement of a new and more profound emphasis on ambiguity and paradox, which will be continued throughout the book, in spite of the fact that the book as a whole is firmly organized and directed. This is in itself disconcerting: we would have expected less paradox than in *Pantagruel,* and we get more. What Rabelais is really doing with the dog

[12] Leo Spitzer has pointed out that this expression was a traditional one in biblical exegesis, and that Rabelais's making it concrete instead of metaphorical is already comic ("Rabelais et les rabelaisants," *SFr* XII (Sept.–Dec. 1960), 401–23).

and the bone is making an elaborate joke at the reader's expense: encouraging him to think the book is full of edifying material and then laughing at him for his credulity.

The first chapter, even more relaxed and chatty in style than the beginning of *Pantagruel,* makes no attempt to improve upon the latter's facetious genealogy but simply refers to it. There is a spurious sort of *vraisemblance* about this: Rabelais is aligning *Gargantua* in the same frame of reference as *Pantagruel,* although the assimilation is false on three counts. First, *Pantagruel* was already a parody and therefore immune from the need for *vraisemblance.* Second, while a genuine genealogical table might inspire confidence, a satirical one would not. And third, Rabelais is pretending at this point that his book is similar in frame of reference to the preceding one, which it is not, as we shall see. This kind of double bluff on the whole subject of *vraisemblance* is more characteristic of *Gargantua* than any of the other books and is worth examining.

At the end of chapter 6 Rabelais comments at some length on the strange birth of Gargantua, who emerged from Gargamelle's left ear like Minerva from Jupiter's head. His first remark is "Je me doubte que ne croyez asseurement ceste estrange nativité," an understatement which gains added force from its contrast to Rabelais's normal habit of overstatement. The next sentence contains the elements of a very fine double bluff: "Si ne le croyez, je ne m'en soucie" (false detachment of the kind already noticed in *Pantagruel*), "mais un homme de bien, un homme de bon sens" (are they necessarily the same thing?), "croit tousjours ce qu'on luy dict et qu'il trouve par escript" (false assimilation and a satirical paradox: the assimilation is false in view of the stress laid all through the novel on the importance of the spoken word and, in general, the danger of the written word—education by word of mouth is better than that culled from books, and so forth). But while it is obvious that only an idiot believes everything he is told, there is a context in which that idiot becomes the authentic wise man—the context of the Gospels—so Rabelais goes on (in the first edition) to quote Solomon and St. Paul and to make a delightfully comic attack on the Sorbonne ("foy est argument des choses de nulle apparence"). This could be taken as sacrilegious and Gargantua's birth as a parody of Christ's, but Rabelais has a covering argument yet to come: nothing is impossible to God; therefore there is nothing antireligious about Gargantua's birth. This whole development is so many-edged that it cuts everybody: the credulous who believe all they are told (by the Sorbonne) even if it's stupid; the freethinkers, who refuse to believe anything strange and so deprive themselves of the divine paradox of the Gospels; the humorless, who have to consider God's place in everything, even in a satirical birth contained in a parody of a parody of the epic; and the pedantic philosophers, who make the actions of God subject to the same laws and restrictions as those of men. I am not convinced, as is Professor Screech, that the emphasis should go on one or the other of these satirical implications; the essential thing is that they are there, all at once contradicting each other but not necessarily canceling each other out.

In chapter 7, again getting at the Sorbonne, Rabelais is more simply lighthearted on the same subject: Scotist philosophers have affirmed that Gargamelle "pouvoit traire de ses mammelles quatorze cens deux pipes neuf potées de laict pour chascune foys," and Rabelais comments simply, "Ce que n'est vraysemblable." But it is not quite clear for whom it is not *vraysemblable,* and the suggestion clearly is that the Sorbonne spends its time condemning propositions which are none of its business.

The question of *vraisemblance* becomes a major preoccupation in *Gargantua* and produces several effects which were not nearly so noticeable in *Pantagruel.* Let us consider first the question of size. Already in the first book the ratio of giant size to ordinary size was variable. In chapter 5 Pantagruel is small enough to play tennis with the students, while in chapter 32 he shelters an army from the rain with his tongue, and his mouth contains cities "non moins grandes que

Lyon ou Poictiers."[13] There is no reason to suppose that this change in ratio is absent-minded; it is obviously deliberate and, in the first book, has two main effects: to make us laugh with surprise at a sudden change in scale and to make us question the validity of our criteria for what is "normal."

In *Gargantua* size is used still more disconcertingly. In chapter 23, during his strenuous physical education, Gargantua runs up the side of a house to a window a lance's length above the ground; later he climbs into trees and up and down the outside of a house fully armed. This is ludicrous, even if the lance is a gigantic one; moreover, in the next paragraph he performs tasks which would need the strength of a giant. In chapter 36 Gargantua has grown so large that he thinks cannonballs are flies; in the same chapter he demolishes a fortress with his stick. This is the only incident during the war in which the giants use their size against the enemy; it seems unfair, but perhaps Rabelais is underlining their virtue by pointing out that they could have ended the war in five minutes if they had wanted to take advantage of their size. Size is not used, in particular, in chapter 48, when one might expect Gargantua to deal with Picrochole's fortress as he dealt with the previous one.

Rabelais's main purpose in all these cases may be simply to vary as much as possible the comic effects to be gained by size; one result of them, nevertheless, is to introduce a disconcerting relativity into our accepted ideas on our world. The success of the comic effects does not need emphasizing: from the destruction of the forests by Gargantua's horse (ch. 16; borrowed from the *grandes chroniques*) to the incident of the pilgrims in the salad (ch. 38) and the gift to Toucquedillon of a chain so enormously heavy that he could not conceivably wear it (ch. 46), Rabelais exploits each and every comic possibility. Apart from fairly frequent passing references, seven chapters of *Gargantua* are mainly concerned with size (7, 8, 16, 17, 36, 37, and 38)—exactly the

---

[13] There are some excellent pages on the ambiguity of size and time in Paris, *Rabelais au futur*, pp. 138–42.

same number as in *Pantagruel*, but the comedy is more varied and ingenious. When he came to write the *Tiers livre*, Rabelais presumably felt that the subject was exhausted, since it is nonexistent there and extremely infrequent in the *Quart livre*. In any case, the constant shifts in size appear to work against *vraisemblance*, which at the same time is emphasized in other ways.

Size is not the only domain in which the register constantly shifts; the same applies to time and place. This needs emphasizing because of the many critical remarks to the effect that Rabelais "forgot" that Gargantua died in Book One or that he had given the *châtellenie de Salmiguondin* to two different people. A man brought up to remember by heart large chunks of what other people had written was not likely to forget so easily what he had written. These contradictions are deliberate and are all part of the techniques of shock.

The relativity of time will become more important in the last two books, but there is one striking case in *Gargantua:* the enormous length of time (fifty-four years) which Gargantua spends studying under Thubal Holoferne. This is such an obvious joke that no one could miss it, but in the later books there will be more subtle manipulations of time which often go unnoticed. In any case, this lack of verisimilitude about time contrasts strikingly with Rabelais's precision in *Gargantua* over place, precision so genuine that detailed maps of the war can be drawn up. This precision is itself in contrast to the fantastic geographical imprecision of Picrochole's councillors (ch. 33), who send him on imaginary campaigns whose itinerary betrays their lack of geographical knowledge. An extension of this technique is the well-known numerical precision ("9876543210 hommes, sans les femmes et petits enfans") in fanciful contexts. Rabelais did not invent this joke, but he uses it throughout the novel, ostensibly to create verisimilitude.

Another essential question related to *vraisemblance* is the place of the author in the story, and it has been noted often enough that Rabelais becomes more and more the self-conscious narrator as the novel develops. Apart from chapter 6, already discussed, Rabelais intervened comparatively little in *Pantagruel*. In *Gargantua* he intervenes a good deal, in different ways and for different reasons. The prologue starts out by establishing a facetious relationship with imaginary readers—*Beuveurs* and *Verolez*—which paradoxically has the effect of widening, not closing, the gap between Rabelais and his actual readers. A rhetorical technique—apostrophe—which is intended to create *vraisemblance* has, in fact, done the opposite.

We have already mentioned an imaginary dialogue between Rabelais and his reader (in ch. 6) which is pure bluff. More common than this in *Gargantua* is the ascribing of verisimilitude to a tall story by pretending to have been an eyewitness: "Je l'ouy une fois appellant Eudemon, depuis la porte Sainct Victor jusques à Montmartre" (ch. 23). Rabelais shares this trick with most of the *conteurs* of his century and, indeed, of any century; how many of one's acquaintance in Europe met personally that nun with hairy arms who was a parachutist in disguise? Throughout the rest of the novel Rabelais will scatter his "je veidz," "j'ay veu," and references to "noz gens," but he does it so frequently, and it is so impossible that his stories could be true, that once again what looks like a technique for producing *vraisemblance* actually destroys it.

This technique, in spite of its apparent obviousness, is one of paradox; the unexpected apostrophe to the reader is a shock technique. It is used in *Gargantua* just often enough to startle and not so often that we become immune to it. We have mentioned the "je me doubte que ne croyez asseurement ceste estrange nativité" of chapter 6, and there is another good example at the beginning of chapter 27. Rabelais describes how Picrochole's soldiers pillaged the plague-ridden houses of Seuillé without catching anything, although the clergy and doctors had all died of the disease. "Dont vient cela, Messieurs? Pensez y, je vous pry." As well as being startling, this is ambiguous—is Rabelais actually apostrophizing his reader, or is he using this incident as an allegory of the religious situation, in which case the *Messieurs* may be the religious leaders of one side or the other? *Pensez y* is also ambiguous, since it can mean simultaneously "Think about it" and "Do something about it."

Rabelais's use of the various techniques of *vraisemblance*, then, reinforces the idea given by the prologue that paradox and surprise effects will be more important in the second book than in the first. But what about ambiguity? We discussed the chapters of *Pantagruel* which could be called parlor-game enigma; only three in *Gargantua* could be put in this category. Chapter 2, the *Fanfreluches antidotées*, is a classic example of *coq-à-l'âne*, in which one is constantly expecting some important hidden meaning to rise to the surface, but the ingenuity of generations of critics has not made sense of much of it.[14] This is what one would expect from the dog/bone passage of the prologue: something that looks like an enigma to be deciphered but has, in fact, no marrow at all.

The case of chapter 5 is very different, and we might say that, following so close upon chapter 2, it constitutes the perfect case of Rabelaisian double bluff. The *Fanfreluches antidotées* looked like sense, or at least looked as though some meaning could be extracted from them, and turned out to be nonsense, while the "Propos des bien yvres" look like a series of unrelated exclamations and statements and turn out to be largely coherent. This is, in fact, a false *coq-à-l'âne* (as Abel Lefranc was the first to point out)[15] but a genuine *énigme,* in which the careful reader can distinguish the remarks made by the different characters and fit them together to form conversations.[16] There may well be a didactic purpose behind this technique: Rabelais, preoccupied with the uses and abuses of the spoken word, is warning us that sense and nonsense are not always what

---

[14] Since I wrote this, I have learned that Professor Edward Morris of Cornell University has a very persuasive theory which does make sense of the *Fanfreluches.* He expounded part of his theory at a Rabelais symposium at SUNY (Albany) in Nov. 1969.

[15] In the critical edition, I (1913), 52.

[16] However, as Jean Paris points out (*Rabelais au futur,* pp. 82–86), Lefranc's solution to the problem of who makes which speech is by no means the only possible one; in fact, any number of different combinations could be made.

they seem. Chapter 5 is, in any case, considerably more ingenious and interesting than most of the enigma chapters of *Pantagruel*.

The same applies to chapter 58, the *Enigme en prophetie,* the only other chapter to be based on enigma in this way. Is it coincidence that the book begins with a paradoxical prologue and ends with an enigma? This ending, in any case, tends to destroy the impression of firm construction given by the rest of the book and, in particular, by the Abbaye de Thélème, a construction in both the physical and the moral sense. The *énigme* is again a double bluff in that we do not know where to put the emphasis; is it a description of civil revolution which represents a tennis game, or a joke description of a tennis game which disguises a serious statement about the plight of the *évangéliques?* In the first case the enigma has two elements, which is certainly all the original author of it, be he Rabelais or Mellin de Saint-Gelais, intended.[17] In the second case it has three, so that one must crack two successive layers of bone to get at the marrow. This interpretation, first put forward by Professor Screech, is tempting,[18] but I still think it more likely that Rabelais is simply demonstrating the possibilities and pitfalls of enigma as a technique.

Less ambiguity than in *Pantagruel* on the plot level, then, but what about the language? I would say that the Rabelaisian sentence is becoming more economical, tighter in construction, and less dispersed and diffuse. Let us compare with our sentence from *Pantagruel* the following sentence from chapter 18 of *Gargantua:* "Maistre Janotus, tondu à la cesarine, vestu de son lyripipion à l'antique, et bien antidoté l'estomac de coudignac de four et eau beniste de cave, se transporta au logis de Gargantua, touchant davant soy troys vedeaulx à rouge muzeau, et trainant après cinq ou six maistres inertes, bien crottez à profit de mesnaige."

This is unfair to some extent because the sentence is much shorter

[17] See R. L. Frautschi, "The 'Enigme en Prophétie' (*Gargantua* LVIII) and the Question of Authorship," *FS* XVII (1963), 331–39.

[18] M. A. Screech, "The Sense of Rabelais' *Enigme en prophétie,*" *BHR* XVIII (1956), 392–404.

and concerns action, not description, but it does contrast strongly, by its symmetry and economy of organization, with the loose structure of the *Pantagruel* sentence. It has a main verb in the middle, preceded by three elements which are mainly description and followed by two which are mainly action and a final one which is descriptive again. The six elements taken in order describe Maistre Janotus from his head to his feet. *Tondu à la cesarine* (i.e., bald) is a typical bathos technique, but whereas in an example like "[il] tyra ses heures de sa braguette" (*G.,* ch. 35) the unexpectedness of the ending simply makes you laugh, here the ending completely negates the beginning. *Tondu à la cesarine* means not *tondu* at all, so this is another example of effort expended to no purpose and really amounts to a periphrasis. The same applies, of course, to *coudignac de four* (bread) and *eau beniste de cave* (wine), with the difference that the juxtaposition of bread and wine, apropos of a theologian, might raise serious implications. Here comes an ambiguous theme again: bread and wine are the elements of the Mass, but they are also generally regarded as the basic necessities of life, so it is only the profession of Maistre Janotus that makes us suspect theological implications here.

These first three elements are symmetrically constructed (*tondu . . . vestu . . . bien antidoté*), and while the first and third are description by negation, the second is genuine description. However, the juxtaposition of the bald head and the theological insignia (in the first edition) creates a comic effect, increased by the fact that more description is lavished on the contents of Janotus's stomach than on the rest of him. The main verb, which is the only regular verb in the sentence, is delightfully intransitive. *Se transporta* is, in fact, ambiguous: Janotus himself would take it as descriptive of the portentous gait suitable to someone of his importance; to us it suggests merely that the size of his stomach prevents him from walking vigorously like other people. The main clause is followed by two symmetrical clauses (*touchant . . . trainant . . .*) which correspond to the three preceding elements except that they are introduced by present instead of past participles. They are further symmetrical in that one refers to *davant soy* and one to *après,* in that each contains a pun (*vedeaulx/inertes*), and in that the verb in each only makes sense when you get to the end of the clause. *Touchant* refers to driving livestock, which is explained by *vedeaulx* (pun on *bedeaux* and so a comparison of a congregation to a herd of cows), which in its turn is amplified by *à rouge muzeau* (they resemble calves because they have red noses, and they have red noses because they drink—a vice traditionally attributed to theologians). In the next clause *trainant* makes some sense when you get to *maistres*—taking the verb metaphorically, he must be dragging them in the sense that they are following unwillingly—but when you get to *inertes,* it makes a different kind of sense, since the verb now becomes literal instead of metaphorical and gives a delightful picture of Janotus dragging quiescent bodies behind him as he walks. Then you realize that *inertes* is a pun (*in artibus*), which makes it metaphorical, which in turn shifts *trainant* back from literal to figurative.

The sentence would have been perfectly symmetrical if Rabelais had stopped it here, but he characteristically adds one more element, thus leaving it slightly lopsided. But by beginning this last clause with *bien crottez,* he refers it back to *bien antidoté* (same adverb, past participle, and a rhyme) and so to the first series of descriptive elements, and also gives a better balance to the central verb by having it preceded and followed by three elements.

There is, then, at least as much to analyze in this sentence as in the much longer one from *Pantagruel.* There is in particular a very remarkable use of verbs: only one main verb, which is passive rather than active, although it indicates movement; a whole collection of past participles which have all kept some active force (*tondu* = *s'étant tondu,* etc.); and two present participles which have no active force in the syntax (both could be replaced by *ayant*) but which have considerable comic ambiguity of meaning. It is ironic anyway to lavish all these verbs upon Janotus, who is one of the most idle and least active (except in words) characters Rabelais created.

This sentence does seem to show a more controlled and directed use of comic techniques than the one from *Pantagruel,* which appeared to rely more on the inspiration of the moment and less on an organized view of the sentence as a unit. I am not claiming that Rabelais consciously intended all the effects I have found in his sentence, but it is significant that they are there, compressed so neatly into such a small space. There is, on the other hand, less diversity of comic technique than in the *Pantagruel* sentence, and fewer of the techniques used have a shock effect. The impression of having to change gear mentally is less frequent, although I think it does happen with *trainant,* for which we make the jump from literal to metaphorical and back to literal.

It would be necessary to analyze more passages from *Gargantua* in more detail in order to make a convincing demonstration, but this one does show, I think, that Rabelais's use of language has changed and that he is employing more compression and symmetry but less ambiguity and fewer shock techniques. One linguistic device does seem more prominent than in the previous book: the comic literal use of expressions which are usually employed metaphorically. This is a very old device, indeed, and the mainspring of many fifteenth-century farces. Rabelais's use of it is discreet by comparison with the *Farce de Pathelin,* for instance, but *Gargantua* provides some first-rate examples. In chapter 12 the expression "avoir le moyne" ("to be made a fool of") is used by the nobles and taken literally by the young Gargantua, who replies, "Je le vous nye. Il ne fut, troys jours a, ceans." In chapter 43 its use is different. When Gymnaste says, "Ilz ont le moyne," he implies two things: first, a grim joke (the enemy have, in fact, captured Frere Jean), and second, a prophecy (because they have the monk, they will be made fools of, as they are in the next chapter). This sophisticated playing on the literal and metaphorical meanings of an expression is much more subtle than Villon's "Laissons le moustier où il est" [19] or Pathelin's "Il aura de l'oie." In chapter 45 Rabelais strikes a further blow for *vraisemblance* by claiming that the metaphorical use of "bailler

[19] In *Le testament* (1461), xxxiv, l. 265.

le moyne" dates from this episode, but once again the claim is so obviously ridiculous that *vraisemblance* is destroyed instead of being encouraged.

The best-known joke of this kind in *Gargantua* is the monks' proposal to sing "contra hostium insidias" while Picrochole's men are attacking the vineyard. The biblical origin of this expression is presumably literal.[20] But the *hostium insidiae* of the litany had come to mean "the wiles of the devil," so it is both appropriate and inappropriate to invoke God's help against them in the case of flesh-and-blood *hostium insidiae*. There is no "bluff" attached to the device in these cases, but Rabelais uses them with the same kind of subtlety which he employs to create ambiguity in other cases.

On the level of plot and general atmosphere, there is also some evolution. We have already discussed his increasingly subtle use of ambiguity; let us consider now the same shock techniques we discussed in *Pantagruel*. We have already mentioned that *Gargantua* divides neatly into three sections, childhood, education, and war, or four sections if one wishes to consider Thélème separately. It is also more symmetrically balanced than *Pantagruel,* in that twenty-eight chapters are mainly comedy of action (4, half of 6, 7, 11, 15, 16, 17, 18, half of 20, 21, 22, 23, 24, 25, 26, 27, 30, 32, 34, 35, 36, 38, 42, 43, 44, 47, 48, 49, and 51) and thirty mainly intellectual or linguistic (1, 2, 3, 5, half of 6, 8, 9, 10, 12, 13, 14, 19, half of 20, 28, 29, 31, 33, 37, 39, 40, 41, 45, 46, 50, 52, 53, 54, 55, 56, 57, and 58). Some of these chapters, particularly in the section on education, are not funny at all, but generally speaking in this book Rabelais achieves a mixture of comedy and satire much more subtle than in *Pantagruel*. The library of St. Victor was such a mixture, but a very obvious one, whereas the scene with Picrochole's evil and stupid councillors (ch. 33) or with Gargantua and the pilgrims in the salad (ch. 38) is a much more delicate combination. And whereas chapter 21 of *Pantagruel* can be divided neatly into two halves, one comedy of

[20] Although Erasmus refers to Psalm 91 (90 in the Vulgate) as "this mystical psalm" (in "Dulce bellum inexpertis").

action and the other linguistic comedy, chapter 6 of *Gargantua* slides imperceptibly from one to the other.

A good example of this disconcerting mixture of *comique* and *sérieux* is chapter 28. It begins with a narration of Picrochole's exploits, followed by a description of Grandgousier seated by the fire which is at the same time comic and moving—comic because of the relationship in size between a giant's *couilles* and a normal fire, and because of the very obvious *b* alliteration in the penultimate clause; moving because of the nostalgia implicit in this picture of the simple father-ruler who in 1534 is a useless anachronism. Then comes the arrival of the shepherd with the news of Picrochole's savage invasion, and the sentence describing his entry is at the same time a breathless indirect report of what he says. In this case the context is tragic, but rendered by a style which is comic, inasmuch as it conveys perfectly the out-of-breath panic which animates the person described. (One notices in passing the very different flavor of *se transporta* in this sentence.)

The same technique is used in Grandgousier's speech of lamentation, and here again it is not sufficient to talk about *fond* versus *forme*. Certain of Grandgousier's exclamations and rhetorical questions ("Holos! holos! . . . Qui le meut? Qui le poinct? Qui le conduict? Qui l'a ainsi conseillé? Ho! ho! ho! ho! ho! . . . Ho! ho! ho! ho! mes bonnes gens . . .") are at the same time comic and tragic, just as his nature is to be comic in his naïveté and imposing in his serious moral purpose. Rabelais has painted a portrait here which has few equals outside his work: the comic evangelical hero. And he has succeeded here where the first book did not. Pantagruel, and even Gargantua in his dilemma at the birth of his son and death of his wife, are tragic or comic in turn; Grandgousier here manages to be both at once.

I have discussed this chapter at length, mainly because its double effects are so subtle that they are not always apparent on first reading. The only disconcerting thing about it is that we are forced to make a sudden shift in perspective from a good but simple-minded giant to an incarnation of the ideal ruler. It is only after making the shift that we can appreciate that for Rabelais these two pictures are not antithetical but coexistent and complementary.

Shifts in atmosphere tend, then, to be less startling than in *Pantagruel,* and the transition from comic to serious is made more subtly. A great deal of good advice, on education, war, government, and religion, is handed out by the giants in the course of the book, but the transition from facetious action to good advice is managed very cleverly. Chapter 39, apart from a couple of facile jokes at the expense of monks, is purely facetious and establishes Frere Jean in his role of exuberant antimonk. Frere Jean is himself an enigma and remains so throughout the three books in which he appears. He is at the same time Rabelais's ideal monk in some ways and his antimonk in other ways. He combines a direct approach to life's problems, and a violent dislike of superstition and hypocrisy, with a gluttonous appetite and a fondness for dubious stories, the aspect most prominent here.

Chapter 45 is a good example of this new subtlety in the combining of comic and serious. It begins in a facetious vein and becomes gradually more and more serious and evangelical in tone. An examination of the themes treated in it shows how skillfully Rabelais interweaves them. They can be conveniently divided into themes of the book as a whole and themes of this particular episode. The general themes are giants, thirst, sickness, sexuality, and speech, and the first thing to strike the reader is that the giant theme is absent (unless he wants to consider the *clochier de l'abbaye* a giant phallic symbol). This absence already indicates that the main import of the chapter will be serious. The thirst theme is present, in the initial *desjeuner,* in Gargantua's refusal to eat and drink because of his worry about the monk, in Frere Jean's opening cry "Vin frays!," in the reference to *hydropiques,* in the abbot Tranchelion *le bon beuveur,* in the water of the Nile, and in the final provision of *bouteilles de vin* for the pilgrims' journey. None of these has anything to do with the thirst theme of folklore recurrent in *Pantagruel,* and the relationship between wine and religion is ambiguous. Wine is recommended for the pilgrims and welcomed by the giant and his companions, but the abbé Tranchelion's drinking habits have presumably ruined his abbey ("Et les moynes, quelle chere font ilz?"), and Frere Jean's constant references to wine are more characteristic of the antimonk than of the ideal monk.

The sickness theme is a central one of the episode, as well as an important one in all four books, and the word *peste* occurs six times in the chapter. The pilgrims are seeking the saint's help against the plague, but at the same time the saint is accused of causing the plague. Several other sicknesses are mentioned, including pox and sterility, which connect to the next theme, but the implication is that the preachers are causing worse moral sickness by their false doctrine (misuse of speech). Sexuality is important here mainly in anticlerical satire, but sterility appears as an erudite subject.

The other central theme of the episode, as of the book, is *la parole.* The chapter begins with two verbal jokes: "avoir le moyne" (see above, pp. 64–65) and "male encontre," a pun on *mâle, mal,* and probably *con.* This is lighthearted, but the subject of the chapter is, in fact, serious: the right use of words. The *faulx prophetes* have told the pilgrims that saints cause illness, because they have themselves been misled by the coincidence of the saints' names. This is an example of the dangerous assimilation between the signifier and the thing signified, to use Jean Paris's language, which is so often attacked by Rabelais and is presented as more dangerous than physical illness ("La peste ne tue que le corps, mais telz imposteurs empoisonnent les ames"). It is as always the *use* of words which is in question; the pilgrims' spokesman, Lasdaller, has a funny name himself which is simply a joke. The misuse of words by the preachers is opposed to the right use of words by Grandgousier, who is seen praying in the first paragraph and who, quoting St. Paul, tells the pilgrims in three sentences all they need to know in order to live Christian lives.

The second group of themes, those particular to this part of the book, comprises war, religion, kingship, and humanism. War is barely mentioned—this is a breathing space between battles. Religion is essential, and this chapter is a good résumé of the evangelical point of view. Rabelais is clearly against pilgrimages, the misguided veneration of saints, the immorality of monks (Frere Jean is not immoral, merely loose-speaking, and has just acquitted himself well in the war), and the dishonesty or stupidity of preachers. He is in favor of direct prayer to God (no Virgin, no saints) and the Christian life according to St. Paul. The distinction between religion and *parole* as themes is an artificial one; they are in many cases identical.

Kingship is an important theme of the whole Picrocholine episode. Here we see Grandgousier in his role as the ideal father of his people, praying for their safety and concerning himself with their problems, and Gargantua as the ideal prince, leading his men to and from war, worrying so much about a companion that he can't eat, and theorizing from Plato's *Republic*. Humanism, finally, is connected with all these themes. Humanist attention to textual authenticity shows up the false superstitions of the pilgrims and teaches that true Christianity is found in St. Paul, not in the Church. Gargantua adduces two learned references to support Frere Jean's anticlerical joke, the false preachers are compared to poets who describe evil gods, and Gargantua quotes Plato on kings and philosophers. Even Frere Jean, generally an anti-intellectual in this book, mentions Proserpine, and in the second half of the chapter there is an interesting mixture of biblical and Classical references.

It is clear from this brief summary that many things are being discussed here, and that they are all being discussed at once. There is no transition from one subject to the next. Important things are said simultaneously about physical and moral illness, speech, war, religion, and kingship, and less important things about wine, sex, and humanism, and they are all interrelated to such an extent that almost every sentence deals with at least two of them. There is nothing sudden or shocking in the chapter, but there is a staggeringly subtle and skillful interweaving of comic and serious, minor and major themes.

Does this attenuation of shock effect mean that Rabelais no longer wishes to startle and disconcert his reader? I don't think so; he simply wishes the surprise to be less immediately shocking and so more liable to convince on a deeper level.

The same sort of change in technique has taken place in the case of another comic device discussed above: the expenditure of energy on trivial pretexts. In *Gargantua* this whole technique has become much more restrained, organized, and positive—controlled exuberance, as opposed to the apparently spontaneous exuberance of the first book. The doctrine of education which Rabelais is advocating did not need four chapters of satire and two of constructive suggestion for its exposition, and it was a fine joke to destroy the traditional ideal of the monastic life not by pulling down an old abbey but by building a new one, complete to the last minute, if not always accurate, detail. But this is not to say that Rabelais has abandoned his earlier use of this technique. Janotus de Bragmardo's speech is a magnificent example (the bells he is begging for have, unknown to him, already been returned), and the character of Frere Jean is the personification of exuberance. Nevertheless, however expansive this exuberance is, it is always displayed with some end in view—saving the wine, satirizing priests, winning the war—and so gratuity is subordinated to purpose, whereas in certain chapters of *Pantagruel* purpose seemed to come second to exuberance for its own sake. The only chapters of *Gargantua* which seem to me to come into this category are 9 and 10, whose only purpose is to caricature etymology.

Disproportionate exuberance is not the only technique Rabelais enjoys playing with. We have seen that *Gargantua* is to some extent a parody of *Pantagruel,* which was a parody of a parody of an epic; these first two books are also at the same time novels and antinovels. The characters are entertaining, we care what happens to them, and there is an interplay of genuine suspense and parody of suspense, particularly in the Picrocholine war. Similarly, the whole Grandgousier-Picrochole struggle is at the same time an obvious allegory (Picrochole = Gaucher de Sainte-Marthe, *or* Charles Quint, *or* the anti-evangelical ruler) and a satire of allegory which picks up the dog/bone theme of the prologue. Rabelais has deliberately chosen a story which can be interpreted in several different ways, as well as being enjoyed for its own sake.

Effects of shock and ambiguity tend to be more subtle than in *Pantagruel,* then, but also more organized and economical. Whereas the first book aimed haphazardly at a random selection of targets, the second has a unified construction and a more positive moral purpose. Of course, exuberance is not wanting, and the introduction and exploits of Frere Jean are at least as vivid and exciting as those of Panurge, but on the whole one can say that bluff is present as part of the structure of the book rather than for its own sake.

BOOK THREE

The *Tiers livre* is a very different kind of book—so different, indeed, that there has never been a book quite like it before or since. The title, *Le tiers livre des faicts et dicts heroiques du bon Pantagruel,* is a fine piece of bluff to start with; not only are there no *faicts heroiques* in the book, not only is it all talk (*dicts heroiques!*) and no action, but it isn't the *tiers livre . . . de Pantagruel* either, since he necessarily did not appear in the second.

The prologue to this book has created more critical problems than almost any other section of Rabelais's works. It begins in much the same way as the *Gargantua* prologue, except that Rabelais added the first two words, "Bonnes gens," after the first edition. *Bon* (like *beau*) in Rabelais is often ironic, and may be assumed to be so here, since it is followed by "Beuveurs" and "Goutteux." On the other hand, *Bonnes gens* might be in contrast to the next two expressions and might stand for the "très illustres et très chevaleureux champions" of the *Pantagruel* prologue. This is a basic bluff technique: in an enumeration how do we tell which elements are in apposition and which in opposition? And if

Bonnes gens is ironic, what are we to make of the *bon Pantagruel* of the title?

The introductory paragraphs of this prologue establish a tone that is simultaneously bantering, highly intellectual, and disconcerting. Alongside the usual jokes ("Si l'avez veu, vous n'aviez perdu la veue"), puns (*vain/vin; lopinant/opiner*), digressions, and enumeration, three basic Rabelaisian themes are stated: wine, sight, and hearing. Wine is the most effective bluff theme Rabelais ever used, and the critical arguments over this prologue would have delighted him. Diogenes lived in a wine-barrel, which he subsequently demolished while imitating the war preparations of the Corinthians; the author is going to roll his barrel while drawing inspiration from his bottle, and help the war effort by distributing wine to any who want it. Leaving aside Lefranc's contention that Rabelais's main reference here is to the defense of Paris in 1536,[21] there are at least three likely interpretations of this theme of wine.

There is the reference, already exploited in the *Gargantua* prologue,[22] to the ancient quarrel between conscientious oil-burning writers who believe in hard work and frivolous wine-drinking writers who rely on inspiration.[23] This aspect of the theme would encourage us to look for explanations of Rabelais's aims and procedures as a writer, and to emphasize, for instance, the analogy between Diogenes' actions with his barrel and Rabelais's verbal exuberance or his professed lack of deliberate construction ("A ce triballement de tonneau, que feray-je en vostre advis? Par la vierge qui se rebrasse, je ne sçay encores"). It is even possible to find in the camel-slave story an apology for grotesque episodes in the book.[24] This strikes me as unlikely, but it can be argued from this particular aspect of the wine theme.

[21] Introduction to the *Tiers livre* in vol. V of the critical edition.
[22] See above, p. 54.
[23] This is Floyd Gray's theory in "Structure and Meaning in the Prologue to the *Tiers livre*," *L'Esprit Créateur* III, no. 2 (Summer 1963), 57–62.
[24] As does Alfred Glauser, *Rabelais créateur* (Paris: Nizet, 1966).

Second, drinking can represent the Renaissance thirst for knowledge and happiness. This interpretation is less popular today than it was
a century ago, but it is quite tenable and would reduce Rabelais's "mes-
sage" to an invitation to enjoy life to the full, physically and intellectually.

Third, there is no doubt that to mention wine in 1546 is to evoke
the many controversies over the Eucharist. Is the wine transformed
into the blood of Christ, or does it merely represent it? Is it necessary
to receive communion under both species, or is bread sufficient for the
common herd? It has been maintained that Rabelais is here firmly
stating his point of view, which is that everyone should receive full
communion if he wishes ("Enfans, beuvez à pleins guodetz") but
should not be obliged to do so ("Si bon ne vous semble, laissez-le").[25]
He is supporting a moderate or Erasmian position against the Ger-
man reformers on the one hand and the fanatical Catholics on the
other ("larves bustuaires" are the monks responsible for burning here-
tics, and "mastins cerbericques" are the Dominicans, *Dominici canes*).

There are yet more possibilities in the wine theme. Mikhail Bakhtin would connect it to the carnival aspect of Rabelais which he considers all-important.[26] What about the neo-Platonist metaphor, which
compares the descent of the soul into the body to a progressive drunkenness? [27] And there are no doubt other possible allusions and connotations. Now it is obvious that Rabelais was aware of all these connotations of the drinking theme, but why, once again, should he have
opted for one and rejected the others? How much more likely it is
that he deliberately plays on them all at once, particularly in view of
the ambiguity of the whole Diogenes episode. Diogenes is clearly making fun of the Corinthians by reducing their warlike actions to the

25 See Walter Kaiser, *Praisers of Folly: Erasmus, Rabelais, Shakespeare* (Cambridge,
Mass.: Harvard University Press, 1963).
26 Mikhail Bakhtin, *Rabelais and His World,* tr. Helene Iswolsky (Cambridge,
Mass.: M.I.T. Press, 1968).
27 See Macrobius, *Commentary on the Dream of Scipio,* Book I, ch. 6.

rolling, and subsequent destruction, of a humble barrel. But the author offers to help the masons in their work and encourage them by producing his *Tiers livre* from the barrel, which will never run dry and in which "bon espoir gist au fond."

The themes of sight and hearing, which will be important in this book, are also touched upon in the prologue. The equating of *veu* with *ouy parler* ("Si veu ne l'avez (comme facilement je suis induict à croire), pour le moins avez vous ouy de luy parler") is surprising in view of the emphasis elsewhere on the distinction between first- and second-hand experience, but the reason is that it is a false antithesis in this case. Since the sight of Diogenes is not possible, we must make do with hearsay. The real point of this third paragraph is Midas's ears, since listening to the story will be the next best thing to seeing it happen. Ears are often emphasized in the novel, and this particular theme is not ambiguous.[28] But with the wine theme Rabelais's deliberate intention is to exploit all the possible connotations, which of course contradict each other as soon as one tries to separate them, and thereby to reduce the reader to a kind of mental fog over the whole subject.

The most interesting point about this prologue is that it is quite unlike the rest of the book and much more like the previous two books. This may be a further example of bluff; the reader is encouraged to think that ambiguity will be similarly treated in this book, when actually it will be treated quite differently.

In the *Tiers livre,* in fact, Rabelais turns from exercise in ambiguity to discussion of it. Ambiguity is one of the main subjects of the book, and its exposition is an element of the Stoic argument that man must grapple with his own problems and make up his own mind.[29] Rabelais works into this theme gradually: chapter 1 is humanist political polemic, chapter 2 states the basic Pantagruel/Panurge antithesis

[28] See my article, "Rabelais and the Comedy of the Spoken Word," *MLR* LXIII (1968), 575–80.

[29] See M. A. Screech, "Some Stoic Elements in Rabelais' Religious Thought," T.H.R., vols. XXIII–XXIV (Geneva: Droz, 1956), *Etudes Rabelaisiennes*, I, 73–97.

and introduces Panurge's satirical praise of debtors, which occupies chapters 3–4. Professor Saulnier has asserted that Panurge should be taken seriously and that he is really pleading for a harmonious society.[30] This is possible, and Panurge certainly recalls Erasmus's dream of harmonious discord between the different elements of society.[31] But most critics agree that the episode is a burlesque *éloge* as practiced by Lucian and the Bernesque poets, and that Rabelais would agree with Pantagruel's condemnation of Panurge.[32] There is no doubt about the delight with which Rabelais expounds his paradox, using all the material which he could possibly contribute to it, but it is basically a joke similar to the Thélème enigma in verse. It also serves to introduce the new Panurge, as long-winded and erudite as his master, and (in ch. 5) the new Pantagruel, who, instead of playing tricks and laughing at dirty jokes, represents the moral arbiter and draws the ethical conclusion. This very sudden change in the protagonists' characters and relative roles warns the reader to expect something different in the plot.

Chapter 6 introduces the marriage theme, on a lofty and erudite plane. This theme is no longer considered by critics to be the basic one, but Panurge's desire to get married does provide the plot, such as it is. In chapter 7 he explains his twofold reason for wanting matrimony: to avoid military service on the one hand and the dangers of illicit love affairs on the other. The intellectual tone of chapter 6 is comic in retrospect, because Panurge's real motives are so very down to earth.

Chapter 8 contains another satirical *éloge*, again by Panurge, this time of the *braguette*. This appears also to be an Erasmian reminiscence: in "Spartam nactus es, hanc orna" (*Adages,* II, v, i) man's lack of natural protection is adduced as evidence that he was intended for mutual love, not mutual war. Rabelais's use of Pliny is thus doubly

[30] V.-L. Saulnier, *Le dessein de Rabelais* (Paris: S.E.D.E.S., 1957).
[31] Erasmus, "Festina lente" (*Adages,* II, i, i).
[32] Jean Paris finds a more fundamental significance in the episode, taking the Marxist view of money as a metaphor for substance (*Rabelais au futur,* pp. 179–84).

paradoxical; is Panurge's argument, however hyperbolic, to be accepted as basically reasonable or denounced as basically wrong, since according to Erasmus war is an unnatural thing? In any case, this reminiscence, coming so close to the other, suggests that Erasmus was definitely in Rabelais's mind as he wrote this book.

In chapter 9 we are at last introduced to Panurge's marriage dilemma, which is the ostensible subject of the central section of the book. The chapter is a fine burlesque of useless conversation between two people who are thinking on different planes and between whom no positive contact is possible. From a philosophical point of view there is no doubt that Screech is right in claiming that Panurge is the fool who refuses to make up his mind and Pantagruel the Stoic wise man who states that the only problem lies in Panurge's will (ch. 10).[33] But other considerations are at work here. This is the beginning of the best use Rabelais ever made of a technique mentioned in connection with the other two books: the extravagant expenditure of energy on a trivial pretext. He will expend thirty-two chapers (9–38 and 45–48) on a pretext which is not even trivial—it is nonexistent. In the first place, Panurge has two questions, not one, as he stubbornly maintains, and the two are on different levels altogether. The first question, "Shall I get married?," could to some extent be answered by debating some of the points he raises in chapter 9 and weighing the resulting arguments against each other. The second question, "Will my wife deceive me?," is the silliest possible question and cannot conceivably be answered by anyone.

In the second place, if Rabelais had wished to discuss marriage seriously, he would have mentioned many other aspects of it, particularly the question of compatibility of character. Is Panurge the right sort of man to be a good husband? What is a good wife like? Only Hippothadée raises these questions. Now it is unreasonable to suppose that because Rabelais never married, he shared Panurge's attitude on

---

[33] See Screech, "Some Stoic Elements"; and *The Rabelaisian Marriage* (London: Arnold, 1958).

what marriage was for; it is much more likely that he shared Erasmus's views on women and marriage.[34] The logical conclusion is that he is not discussing marriage at all, and the whole plot structure is based on a logically outrageous piece of bluff.

The ambiguity used in the *Tiers livre* is of several different kinds. To begin with, there is plenty of straightforward obscurity, which should not be confused with ambiguity. We may have difficulty understanding Her Trippa's enumeration of methods of divination (ch. 25) or Bridoye's legal quotations (chs. 39–42), but we know that any ambiguity arises from our lack of knowledge, and a sixteenth-century reader would be in the same position unless he happened to be a specialist in these two fields. These two episodes are similar in principle to that of the library of St. Victor and may be evidence of a desire to annoy the reader but not deliberately to confuse him.

But the extraordinary amount of erudition in this book is more than just an elaborate intellectual joke at the reader's expense. It is used to illustrate one of the *Tiers livre*'s basic themes: the question of moral and intellectual authority and how it works. Her Trippa and Bridoye are examples of a type of authority which, while valid in its own field, is too narrowly technical to be helpful on a general plane, and it is at this point that real ambiguity becomes apparent. From a common-sense point of view, why should Her Trippa answer Panurge's second question? It is not a genuine question; moreover, Panurge's insulting attitude does not encourage serious discussion of his problems. But we are left with the impression that Her Trippa is being laughed at—he resembles a machine that cannot be stopped, as Bergson would put it, and he is so far removed from real life that he could not "divine" what his wife was doing behind his back. As in the Thaumaste episode already discussed, Rabelais is making fun of both protagonists, who are both wrong to some extent, and the ambiguity arises from uncertainty over which aspect should be emphasized.

[34] See, for instance, the colloquies "Courtship," "Marriage," "The New Mother," and "The Unequal Match."

But Her Trippa's answer to Panurge's questions is perfectly clear, and this raises a more general problem. We would expect Rabelais to object to some of the consultations—Virgilian lots, dreams, occult methods of divination, the Sybil's leaves, the dumb man, and the idiot —on the ground that their pronouncements are ambiguous and can be interpreted either way, as Montaigne will object to "le parler obscur, ambigu et fantastique du jargon prophetique" ("Des prognostications," I, xi). This is not what happens; in nearly every case the pronouncement is clear, and in every case Pantagruel gives the most sensible interpretation, which is always the same: you will be cuckolded, beaten, and robbed by your wife. The only method of consultation Rabelais condemns is the use of dice, and there is no reason to deny his belief in the possible efficacy of the others. He seems to be explaining that ambiguity, like so many other things, is not what it appears to be, and that outward obscurity does not necessarily imply confusion of content.

Individual episodes confirm this. We have already noticed that the "Propos des bien yvres" conceals coherence behind a mask of incoherence, and several chapters of the Tiers livre use the same technique. Frere Jean's reply to Panurge (ch. 28) looks at first like a parody of a scholastic argument with half the premises left out, but, in fact, each ergo clause is simply a logical result of "Si tu es coqu," and Frere Jean is saying, "What is all the fuss about?" A cuckold has all sorts of very tangible advantages ("une belle femme, des amis beaucoup") and should be a happy man. The ambiguity arises from the clause "tu sera saulvé," which, coming from Frere Jean, might have Christian overtones (you will be saved because you will have had an excellent opportunity to practice the Christian virtues of resignation and humility).

The other counselor who appears at first to be ambiguous is Trouillogan (ch. 36). It may be that Rabelais is poking fun at a certain type of philosopher, and some of Trouillogan's replies ("Ne l'un ne l'aultre, et tous les deux ensemble," to the question "Estes vous marié ou non?") look purely farcical. But as Screech has pointed out, he does make one very pertinent reply.[35] When Panurge asks him, "Que doibs je faire?" his answer is "Ce que voudrez," which is to say (in Stoic terms) : you must make your own decision and do what you *will* to do. In the light of this, remarks like the one previously quoted take on a different meaning; Trouillogan may be referring to the sort of discussion on what constitutes matrimony which Pantagruel has just mentioned in the previous chapter ("avoir et n'avoir femme"). As Trouillogan's modern counterpart, Professor Joad, would have said, it all depends on what you mean by marriage.

The lack of ambiguity in the advice Panurge receives is emphasized by the one genuinely ambiguous episode: the bells of Varennes (chs. 27 and 28). The bells at first seem to say "Marie toy" and then change to "Marie poinct." But the ambiguity arises from Panurge's state of mind, not from any actual change in the sound of the bells, and there are two morals: do not consult bells, and approach your consultation objectively and with an open mind.

In the case of this group of consultants, then, we are given not ambiguous conclusions (though those of the Sybil, Raminagrobis, Nazdecabre, and Triboullet look ambiguous) but a discussion on the nature of ambiguity in the field of knowledge and authority. In no other book does Rabelais assemble such a volume of knowledge on such varied subjects. He parades his familiarity with, among other things, military strategy and principles (ch. 1), medieval physiology (chs. 3–4), Mosaic law (ch. 6), Pliny's principles of botany (chs. 8 and 49–52), Classical theories about lots (chs. 10–12), dreams (chs. 13–14) and oracles (chs. 16–18 and 24), Erasmus's views on monks (ch. 22), demonology (ch. 23), different methods of divination (ch. 25), St. Paul's attitude to matrimony (ch. 30), Galen's medical theories (chs. 31–34), legal procedure (chs. 39–44), and the contemporary controversy about marriage without parental consent (ch. 48). The encyclopaedic character of the book has not been sufficiently stressed, nor has the reason that it is comic.

[35] See Screech, *The Rabelaisian Marriage*.

Most of this erudition is correct and orthodox, but it is all displayed with a view to answering Panurge's question about cuckoldry, which, even if sensible, would be a human and not an intellectual one. Encyclopaedic knowledge is in this context doubly comic, first because it is irrelevant to the question and second because the question is not genuine.

The other group of consultants—Frere Jean, Hippothadée, Rondibilis, and Trouillogan—seems likely to produce more relevant answers. There are two main differences between the two groups. The first group's answers are identical, whereas each member of the second group gives a different one and delivers it verbally. In the first group the answers of the lots, the Sybil, and Raminagrobis are written, Her Trippa's is quoted, and those of Nazdecabre and Triboullet are mainly gesture. This is what we would expect from Rabelais's emphasis elsewhere on the importance of the spoken word and first-hand experience. The answers of the second group are all valid on their own terms. Frere Jean says that cuckoldry is inevitable (except by the use of the rather impractical remedy suggested to Hans Carvel) but is, in fact, more of an advantage than a disadvantage. Hippothadée says that if you choose a wife and govern her and yourself according to St. Paul's precepts, you will be safe. Rondibilis says that the best way to avoid cuckoldry is to trust your wife, not suspect her. And Trouillogan says that since the results of your actions are in the hand of God, the main thing is to make up your mind and stick to it (exactly the same advice as that given by Pantagruel in ch. 10). Panurge could not simultaneously act on all this advice, but any one item of it might help him solve his problem. It would seem, then, that the spoken word is the answer; it is still authority speaking, to be sure, but authority making an effort to adapt itself to the context and apply to a specific problem.

Unfortunately, this optimistic conclusion is completely negated by Pantagruel's speech at the beginning of chapter 19, when he is proposing that Panurge consult the dumb Nazdecabre. In this speech, which is full of Classical references and examples, he says that the most truthful oracles were neither spoken nor written because in both cases errors were possible: "Tant à cause des amphibologies, equivocques et ob-scuritez des mots, que de la briefveté des sentences." The most certain and unambiguous judgments are those given by signs. Later on in this chapter Pantagruel asserts that it is a fallacy to postulate a "languaige naturel." Language is a convention, and "les voix [mots] ne signifient naturellement, mais à plaisir." This is, of course, a very old debate, but Rabelais's remarks here on language undoubtedly undermine the ap-parent efficacy of the verbal consultations.

We were able to divide the chapters of the first two books, by means of their content, into comedy of action and comedy of language. In the *Tiers livre* no such division is possible. Action has become ver-bal, and instead of words describing action, we have words describing words. Whereas action and enigma were separate elements in *Gar-gantua* and *Pantagruel,* here enigma is both the subject of the book and the main comic element of the plot.

This very startling shift in tone is further emphasized by the re-tention of many elements and techniques already used in the other books. Certainly the giant theme has disappeared, but the thirst theme is still present, and chapter 51 picks up both the *Pantagruel* folklore motif (people being hanged complain "de ce que Pantagruel les tenoit à la guorge") and the ambiguous drinking invitation of the prologue ("le noble Pantagruel ne print oncques à la guorge, sinon ceulx qui sont negligens de obvier à la soif imminente"). We have already men-tioned the *éloge des debteurs* as a fine example of effort expended on a trivial pretext, and the Pantagruélion chapters are equally exuberant, besides adding to the book's symmetry. An *éloge satirique* at each end, and in the middle a series of consultations with no intelligent pre-text: an antinovel if ever there was one.

Rabelais has not abandoned the author's intervention in the story (chs. 17, 49, and 50) or the attempt to reassure the reader that the story is true (ch. 51)—though it is perhaps significant that most of these ex-amples occur at the end of the book—or the disconcerting shifts in time and story continuity. Frere Jean, who would be too old to join Pantagruel's companions, suddenly appears without explanation in chapter 13, and Gargantua, who presumably died in chapter 23 of *Pantagruel,* enters with equal suddenness in the middle of chapter 35. Jokes and puns still abound, like "un clystere barbarin" in chapter 34 (*barbarin* evokes at the same time *rhubarbe* and *barbare*).

There is no doubt, however, that many of these comic effects are less frequent and less striking than in the previous books. Display of erudition in all its forms, from the exact (Rondibilis) to the fantastic (Bridoye), is the main comic device. One comic theme, however, is more emphasized than in the other two books.

We have discussed examples of the apparent enigma which turns out to be quite clear. An extension of this technique is the apparent nonsense which turns out to be sensible. The "Propos des bien yvres" is to some extent an example of this, and the *Tiers livre* provides a better one—the story of Seigny Joan in chapter 37. The moral of this story is that the professional fool's judgment on a difficult case was more intelligent than that of the legal experts. This applies to the theme of authority—the layman who has no authority comes off best—and also to a theme which is basic to the *Tiers livre,* that of folly.

This is another fundamentally ambiguous theme, like the wine theme. Seigny Joan turns out to be the most intelligent person present. In chapter 18 Panurge rejects Epistemon's reliance on the authority of Propertius, Tibullus, Porphyry, and Eustathius with the brusque remark, "Vous me alleguez de gentilz veaulx. Ilz feurent folz comme poëtes, et resveurs comme philosophes." According to him, the representatives of intellectual authority are the fools. However, since Panurge himself is a fool, we are presumably not intended to take his remark seriously. But the whole question of Panurge's role in the story is still disputed. At least three recent critics have attempted to "rehabilitate" Panurge,[36] and Kaiser's theory is an interesting one: the

<hr>

[36] Mario Roques, "Aspects de Panurge," in *François Rabelais: ouvrage publié pour le 4e centenaire de sa mort,* T.H.R., VII (Geneva: Droz, 1953), 120–30; Kaiser, *Praisers of Folly;* and Paris, *Rabelais au futur.*

Pantagruel/Panurge antithesis is not between the Stoic wise man and the fool but between Erasmian reason and natural understanding, with Panurge as the fool who cannot quite reach the status of a Fool in Christ.[37] Kaiser's whole argument is ingenious, but I cannot agree that Panurge represents "natural wisdom"—he is a fool on all counts. Nor is he the antithesis of learned; his erudition in the *Tiers livre* is well up to the general level, in spite of his poor opinion of poets and philosophers.

Kaiser maintains that all the characters in the *Tiers livre* are fools except Gargantua, and this is largely true. Some are idiots, some are so narrowly specialized that they are fools outside their own field, and some are so sensible that the foolish world considers them fools. Raminagrobis and Hippothadée are close to being Fools in Christ. But Frere Jean, Epistemon, and Pantagruel are not fools in any sense, and Panurge is a fool in every sense except the Christian one. Rabelais was well aware that, on this question of folly, Stoicism and Christianity, at one on so many other points, come into direct conflict. Screech thinks that Rabelais is attempting to reconcile them; I think it much more likely that he is deliberately exploiting their differences and showing just how many sides there are to the question of folly.

Paradox and ambiguity, then, are given an entirely new treatment in the *Tiers livre*. There is less emphasis on the verbal forms of bluff than in the first two books, less emphasis on individual bluff techniques, but paradox has expanded until it has become the pretext and basic theme, as well as the main comic device, of the book. The marriage problem is ambiguous and forms the core of the book, preceded and followed by a paradoxical *éloge*. The plot, which is simply a list of people consulted with no logical development and no internal structure, has a beginning but no end. The people consulted are mostly fools, but on very different levels, so that the reader must change gear

---

[37] This is, basically, the point of view of Saulnier and Screech. The best argument for the thesis that Rabelais is condemning Panurge is Panurge's misuse of his Classical and biblical authorities. See Screech, *The Rabelaisian Marriage*, and notes to his edition of the *Tiers livre*, T.L.F. (Geneva: Droz, 1964).

mentally between one chapter and another. The value of the advice given varies constantly in tone and relevance. The book as a whole may be about marriage, folly, authority, or ambiguity, or one or all of these things may be simply the pretext for what is in effect an anti-book. The fact that Rabelais chose to write such a book is sufficient proof that ambiguity was one of his major preoccupations.

BOOK FOUR

Any educated reader of the first three books must have awaited the fourth with bated breath—what on earth would Rabelais do next? After the antinovel, in which direction would he turn? What he did was to produce a book that looks much more like the first two than the third, since it is an adventure story, but that continues the *Tiers livre* by being a different kind of antinovel. Once again it is a question of pretext; Panurge's quest has no evolution, no structure, and no end, and the pretexts for the different episodes vary from the fantastic to the nonexistent. This aspect of the book recalls the *Tiers livre,* while the episodic satire and contemporary references recall *Gargantua.* The *Quart livre* is thus a fusion of Rabelais's most important techniques in the preceding books.

With the epistle to Odet de Chastillon he emphasizes a theme which had not been in evidence since the prologue to *Pantagruel,* that of illness and medicine. This is the passage he chose to keep from the 1548 prologue, while abandoning the passage about the breviary, which would have tied up very nicely with the Silenus from the *Gargantua* prologue. Certainly the other prologues refer to *vérolés et goutteux,* but this is the first time the subject of medicine is treated at such length.

This epistle is a defense of the first three books, on two counts: first, that "folastries joyeuses" are "le subject et theme unicque d'iceulx livres," and second, that the books are intended as medicine for the sick, just as the doctor's bedside manner must include conversation intended to "resjouir [le malade] sans offense de Dieu." This analogy is not quite as straightforward as it appears. Rabelais is a doctor, so that to compare himself to a doctor seems curious; moreover, the idea of medicine necessarily includes a "nasty-stuff-but-it's-good-for-you" attitude which would be in opposition to simple *folastries joyeuses*. The two pretexts do not quite dovetail.

The medical theme persists in the 1552 prologue, which is the best one Rabelais wrote from the point of view of construction and logical development. He begins with a much shorter and more dramatic address to the reader: "Gens de bien" (which presumably includes all the different categories of people mentioned in the other prologues), "Dieu vous saulve et guard!" This pious wish is immediately contradicted by "Où estez vous? Je ne vous peuz veoir," which may be simply an introduction to the joke about spectacles but definitely implies that *gens de bien* are difficult to see because there are not too many of them around.[38] This suspicion is reinforced by the recurrence, at the beginning and end of this prologue, of *bon,* which is used in several different contexts: religious ("le bon Dieu"), technical ("bonne vinée"), or simply colloquial ("cela est bon"). We have already mentioned that *bon* and *beau* are often used ironically by Rabelais, and the more often *bon* is repeated, the more ironic it sounds, although there is no reason to assume it would be so in any one of these three cases.

This prologue's main theme is *santé,* one aspect of which (sanity as distinct from health) is *mediocrité,* the moral of the Couillatris story. This story contains subplots in the form of discussions of the gods and their problems, which in turn include contemporary references like the Ramus-Galland quarrel. The whole thing is so well constructed that we do not at first perceive the comic contradictions which underlie it.

---

[38] This is Tahureau's interpretation of the passage in his *Premier dialogue du Democritic,* published in 1565 (ed. F. Conscience (Paris, 1870), p. 71). Le Democritic is criticizing as idealistic Cicero's definition of the orator as "vir bonus et dicendi peritus," since he doubts that a *vir bonus* exists: "Je ne sçay où il s'en pourra trouver un tant parfait auquel on puisse seulement attribuer . . . la premiere partie de cette definition, j'en prendray à tesmoin nostre non moins docte que facetieux Rabelais, disant en ces mots, Gens de bien, Dieu vous sauve et gard, où estes vous, je ne vous peus voir."

The first of these contradictions concerns God. We naturally assume, at the outset, that "le bon Dieu" is the Christian God, or perhaps
more specifically the evangelical God, since he is referred to a few paragraphs later as "[le] benoist Servateur," an expression often used in
Protestant circles. This assumption is confirmed by the whole first section, which progresses from Galen and Asclepiades on health, to God,
who will grant us health as he granted the reasonable wishes of
Zachaeus and of the woodcutter in 2 Kings, chapter 6. But the main
protagonist of the central story is Jupiter, and he and the other gods
are presented as comic in several different ways. First, Jupiter is not
omnipotent but is subject to Fate and must return the lost axe ("Cela
est escript es destins, entendez vous?"). Then he is absent-minded
("Quand? Qui estoient ilz? Où feut ce?") and does not take his re-
sponsibilities very seriously ("Nous y aurons du passetemps beaucoup"). The gods all speak colloquially, and in adjacent paragraphs
two similes reduce them to subhuman stature: they all burst out laughing "comme un microcosme de mouches," and Jupiter frowns majes-
tically while "contournant la teste comme un cinge qui avalle pillules."
In the next paragraph a very similar comparison describes Couillatris
trembling with joy "comme un renard qui rencontre poulles esguarées."
These similes tend to equate Jupiter and Couillatris, who are only sep-
arated by the physical distance between the trapdoor of heaven and
the village of Gravot.

Does all this tend to cast doubts on the omnipotence of the God
appealed to at the beginning and the end of the prologue, or does it
suggest that Jupiter and God are two different names for the same
being? This is tempting, especially since Rabelais brings Aesop's story
up to date by making Couillatris a native of Gravot and by discussing
contemporary problems. But his references to God are very similar to
others in the earlier books, and in spite of the facetiously conversational
context there is no reason to doubt the point of view expressed here.
There is even a distinct moral: "De qui estez vous apprins ainsi dis-
courir et parler de la puissance et praedestination de Dieu, paouvres

gens?" This would suggest a possible equation not between Jupiter and God but between paganism and Calvinism, both of which rely on predestination, though on different planes. Or the moral may simply be that it is futile to argue about free will and fate; we must accept God's word or we shall be embroiled in insoluble problems like the one Jupiter had with the magic fox and dog. Couillatris is rewarded because he did not try to make himself out as anything other than what he was.[39]

The ambiguous status of the gods is balanced by the erotic equivocation which is the basis of the whole episode. Everyone was aware that *coingnée* had two meanings, and Priapus's lengthy explanation of the joke is not really necessary. But this erotic joke connotation, added to Couillatris's name and the quite unequivocal description of Priapus before his first speech, tends to imply that the whole episode is just a rude joke. As we have seen, this is not so, and the moral ("Soubhaitez doncques mediocrité") would be acceptable to Aristotelians and Christians alike, so this is another example of sense which looks like nonsense.

Another very interesting aspect of this prologue will be important in the *Quart livre.* The Ramus-Galland episode may well have arisen from the fact that they are both called Pierre. This suggested the joke about being turned to stone and the association with Pierre du Coingnet, whose name connects this story to the one about the *coingnée.* Similarly, the Couillatris story is basically an illustration of the well-known principle of the golden mean; since Couillatris observes the mean, he literally gets the gold. This is not only a good joke, it is the basic creative technique for many *Quart livre* episodes, as we shall see.

Our first impression is that this book is not at all like the *Tiers*

---

[39] Rabelais is by no means the first Renaissance humanist to use the role of Jupiter in a moralizing context. In Vives's *Fabula de homine* (c. 1520; English translation in E. Cassirer, P. O. Kristeller, and J. H. Randall, Jr., eds., *The Renaissance Philosophy of Man,* 2nd ed. (Chicago: University of Chicago Press, 1950), pp. 387–93) Jupiter has created the world and man as an after-dinner entertainment for the gods. Man resembles Jupiter, can impersonate him perfectly, and acts many parts so well that he is admitted to the audience and to the banquet of the gods.

livre. It is an adventure story, recounting a quest undertaken with a definite purpose and containing constant incident, excitement, and suspense. But is it? In fact, as Leo Spitzer has pointed out, the entire action is gratuitous.[40] One cannot take seriously Gargantua's dispatching a fleet of twelve ships, expensively equipped, plus his only son and favorite companions, in search of the answer to a silly question posed by Pantagruel's ne'er-do-well friend. The marriage problem was a foolish pretext for a series of weighty consultations; it is still more foolish as the reason for a long and dangerous journey, especially when Pantagruel's own marriage problem has just been settled in three lines (*T.l.,* ch. 48). The other possible pretext, Pantagruel's desire to "tous jours veoir et tous jours apprendre" (*T.l.,* ch. 47), is also specious. He certainly sees many things in the *Quart livre,* but the only episode which could remotely be regarded as educational is that of the Macraeons.

Like its predecessor, then, the *Quart livre* is based on a trivial or nonexistent pretext. Is it an adventure story at all? Certainly it owes a certain amount to genuine epics (the *Odyssey* and the *Aeneid*) and to genuine accounts of voyages like Jacques Cartier's. But it also owes a good deal to Folengo, whose *Baldo* is at the same time an anti-epic and a genuine epic.[41] In fact, it has much less action and incident than Folengo—so little, as we shall see, that it represents a different kind of antinovel, the adventure story without adventures. Let us consider first those episodes which appear to be wholly or mainly action. The first surprise is that there are only two—the storm and the encounter with the whale—and in both cases the action is not as straightforward as we expect.[42]

In the storm episode (chs. 18–24) nearly all of this action is conveyed in conversation, either in Panurge's terrified lamentations or in Frere Jean's exhortations to the sailors. A good deal of it, moreover, is

[40] Spitzer, "Rabelais et les rabelaisants," p. 410.

[41] *Opus Merlini Cocaii, poetae Mantuani, Macaronicorum* (Venice, 1520). It is most accessible in the 1605 French version, *Histoire Maccaronique de Merlin Coccaie,* ed. G. Brunet and P. L. Jacob (Paris, 1876). See, most recently, Marcel Tetel, "Rabelais and Folengo," *CL* XV (1963), 357–64.

[42] For the Andouilles episode, see below, p. 95.

conveyed by means of abstruse technical terms which most of Rabelais's contemporaries would have found as puzzling as we do. Not only is there a fantastic collection of nautical terms drawn from different languages and dialects, but the description of the beginning of the storm (ch. 18) is simply an enumeration of Greek terms taken straight out of Aristotle. Is Rabelais replacing the battle-of-the-gods convention, as used by Folengo, for instance, with a convention of his own? To what extent can this paragraph be regarded as an effective description of a storm breaking?

There is no doubt, in any case, about the dramatic qualities of the storm itself, and Rabelais's originality is obvious as soon as his episode is compared with Erasmus's colloquy "Naufragium," on which it is based. There is more actual excitement in "Naufragium"—the ship breaks up, the lifeboat overturns, many are drowned and a few dramatically saved—and it is all described. In Rabelais's scene there is much less dramatic event but a great deal of suspense, conveyed almost exclusively through conversation.

But action is, in fact, the subject of this episode, as Epistemon makes clear in chapter 23. Panurge demonstrates several basic faults of character during the storm—cowardice and superstition in particular—but the most important one is precisely his refusal to act, to be a "fellow-worker with God" like the others.[43] His conversation, while providing description of the others' action, is evidence of his own refusal to act. So this episode is a double paradox very similar to much of the *Tiers livre:* real action is conveyed indirectly by conversation instead of directly by description, and conversation is also presented as a refusal of action.

The encounter with the Physetere (chs. 33–34) is the only other episode of genuine action in the book, and here, too, appearances are deceptive. The only straightforward description of action occurs in the first two paragraphs of chapter 33 and the last two of 34. Panurge's fear again provides indirect description, and most of 34 contains Clas-

43 Cf. Screech, *L'évangélisme,* ch. III.

sical parallels to Pantagruel's prowess. At the beginning of chapter 34 two simple sentences—"Frere Jan ne se y espargnoit. Panurge mouroit de paour"—are evocative only because they recall the storm episode, of which this opposition between Frere Jean and Panurge was the basis.

No other episode in the book (and there are twenty altogether) is even mainly concerned with action. There is action, to be sure, in the Chiquanous and Villon stories, but they are simply stories, removed in time and having nothing to do with either the quest or Panurge's problem. The actual encounter with the Chiquanous is summarily dealt with in chapter 16 and is much less exciting than the preceding chapters of description. In all other cases the interest lies in ambiguity or in words, most often in both.

To return for a moment to the beginning of the book, the reader is alerted by the first adventure (ch. 2) that he is not dealing with epic action. The first port of call is Medamothi (i.e., Nowhere), and naturally enough in Nowhere nothing happens. The basic joke is developed in the list of pictures bought in Medamothi, which are mainly of things which cannot possibly be represented pictorially: Philomela's description to Procne of how she was raped by Tereus, Plato's Ideas, Epicurus's atoms, a portrait of Echo. Even the first two items are jokes of a similar kind; how do you distinguish the "visage d'un appellant" from anyone else's face, since what characterizes an apellant is precisely his appeal? The same applies to "un varlet qui cherche maistre"—the only way to tell that this is what he is doing is by listening to him.

So the adventures begin with a port of call named Nowhere, in which pictures of unrepresentable things are for sale. This is followed by a learned disquisition on carrier pigeons (ch. 3) and two Ciceronian letters (chs. 3 and 4), which recall the letters of the first two books. There is nothing intrinsically comic about them, but they are disconcerting in a context of pseudo-epic and following an episode of facetious fantasy.

The meeting with the merchants (ch. 5) is the pretext for a sly poke at the Council of Trent and a pun on *lanternes,* and it forms the introduction to the Dindenault episode (chs. 5–8). This episode owes a good deal to Folengo, and the bargaining scene, which is not in Folengo, may well be a theatrical recollection.[44] In the *Farce du marchand de pommes,* for instance, there is a similarly comic scene between two women and a merchant who has eggs and apples to sell; when they ask him about the eggs, he praises the apples, and vice versa.[45] Rabelais's scene is much more developed and constitutes the most dramatic conversation in his novel, with the possible exception of the Trouillogan-Panurge one in the *Tiers livre.* In this episode, as in the *Tiers livre,* conversation becomes action, but here it also leads to action—the very dramatic drowning of the sheep and the merchants. Dindenault's only crime appears to be irrelevance, and he is aptly punished by having to listen to Panurge's irrelevant harangue while he drowns (ch. 8). The action/conversation equation is underlined by the fact that the first conversation is given in full, but Panurge's revenging diatribe is merely summarized in reported speech. And, as in the storm scene, all the drama of the bargaining is presented verbally.

Each episode so far has entailed a complete change of tone from the preceding one. Chapter 9 is based, like chapter 2, on a verbal joke, here the neo-Platonic *amours d'alliance.* Rabelais confuses the issue by calling the island Ennasin, which suggested to Lefranc the Esquimaux described by Cartier,[46] and to Marichal the sect of Essenians.[47] It is impossible to be sure that Rabelais intended this ambiguity, and the episode is in itself straightforward. In almost all cases the *alliance* is suggested by a colloquial expression, and the chapter is simply an enumeration of these *alliances.* The first sentence of the Potestat's speech provides one of the best examples in Rabelais of excessive attention given to a trivial subject: "Vous aultres gens de l'aultre monde, tenez pour chose admirable que, d'une famille Romaine (c'estoient les

---

[44] See Folengo, *Histoire Maccaronique,* Book XII.
[45] In Leroux de Lincy and Francisque Michel, *Recueil de farces* . . . (Paris, 1837), vol. III.
[46] Abel Lefranc, *Les navigations de Pantagruel* (Paris: H. Leclerc, 1905), ch. VI.
[47] Robert Marichal, "L'attitude de Rabelais devant le néoplatonisme et l'italianisme," in *François Rabelais* (see note 36), pp. 181–209.

Fabians), pour un jour (ce feut le tresieme du moys de Febvrier), par une porte (ce feut la porte Carmentale, jadis située au pied du Capitole, entre le roc Tarpéian et le Tybre, depuis surnommée Scelerate) . . ." and so on. There are five parentheses altogether, each containing useless minutiae of information which have nothing to do with the matter in hand and merely slow down the sentence. This is a charming parody of the pedantic oratorical parenthesis or, indeed, of the scholarly footnote.

Once again only Spitzer saw the real importance of this episode for Rabelais's novel technique.[48] In the *alliances* words, and, moreover, words normally used metaphorically, have acquired literal, concrete reality. This is first of all a commentary on colloquial usage. Rabelais startles us by taking clichés literally and making them into people, and the absurdity of the result shows us how basically meaningless our clichés are. But at the same time it is a commentary on the creative power of words, since out of the clichés comes an entertaining and colorful episode.

Before we pursue this question of language, let us look for a moment at some other important episodes. The main point of chapters 25–28 is still not clear, in spite of all the critical argument on the subject.[49] Are they a tribute to Guillaume de Langey, for whom a solemnly Classical context was appropriate? A defense of the belief in portents and omens? A cleverly veiled Pan/Christ allegory, attempting to reconcile two very different religious points of view? In any case, Rabelais composed his Pan story (ch. 28) from a mixture of sources and must have been well aware of the possible ambiguity of his version. It would not be surprising, in fact, if ambiguity were the main point here, in which case the passage is intended as an *énigme*. Once again this episode contains no action and has nothing to do with the quest for the *Dive Bouteille*.

[48] Spitzer, "Rabelais et les rabelaisants," p. 413, note 1.
[49] See, in particular, M. A. Screech, "The Death of Pan and Heroes," *BHR* XVII (1955), 36–55; and A. J. Krailsheimer, *Rabelais and the Franciscans* (Oxford: Clarendon Press, 1963), Part II, ch. 11.

Quaresmeprenant is another delightfully obscure personage and makes one think, as Tetel has remarked, of a Bosch painting. It is clear that Rabelais is satirizing fanatical Catholics, devoted to the letter of the law, but most of Xenomanes' description is far from clear, and none of the critical attempts to make sense of it are very convincing. However, if one looks closely at his most important members and attributes, it is clear that he has not much brain ("la cervelle en grandeur, couleur, substance et vigueur semblable au couillon gauche d'un ciron masle"); that he has "l'imagination, comme un quarillonnement de cloches," "L'entendement, comme un breviaire dessiré," and "Les intelligences, comme limaz sortans des fraires"; that his eyes and ears are closed, as one would expect from bigotry; and that "s'il parloit, c'estoit gros bureau d'Auvergne." Most of this fantastic description is simply entertaining, but it is worth noting that it is not technically description at all, but analogy. Having given us in the storm episode action which is not really action, Rabelais here gives us description which is not really description. This is emphasized by the contrast with the following direct description of Physis and Antiphysie.

The Papimanes are also inspired by anti-Catholic satire, and there is a paradox in their basic attitude. By tacitly omitting the *quasi* from the description of the pope as "quasi Deus in terris," they have replaced God with the pope.[50] This kind of mental process, which in Bridoye's case was a harmless aberration, is here shown as a dangerous one, although its results are entertaining for the travelers. There is nothing ambiguous about the satire on the Church's greed and on the abuse of images and superstition in general.

It has been assumed that the Papefigues must also have a contemporary significance, and the most likely suggestion is a reference to the massacre of the Vaudois in 1545.[51] But it would be just like Rabelais to juxtapose the Papefigues and Papimanes, with their similarly formed names, as though to suggest that they are two halves of the same pic-

[50] Screech, *L'évangélisme,* ch. V.
[51] Raymond Lebègue, "Rabelaesiana," *BHR* X (1948), 159–68.

ture, when in fact they are not remotely connected. The Papefigue peasant and the little devil are delightful characters, but they belong to the age-old *conte* tradition rather than to religious polemic. And the episodes are contrasted in other ways. The interest of the Papefigues lies in a story most of which took place some time ago; the Papimanes episode is in the present. There is plenty of action in the Papefigues, even if retrospective, while the Papimanes passage is nearly all talk. So there is really nothing but the names to suggest that these two episodes should be assimilated.

The basis of the Gaster chapters (57–62) is another paradoxical *éloge* on the lines of the *debteurs et emprunteurs* or Pantagruélion, which sets out to prove that hunger is responsible for human progress— not a particularly original paradox. As usual, starting from a simple paradox, Rabelais has drawn a picture of an autonomous little world, acting according to its own laws and containing its peculiar characters related to Gaster. There is a suggestion of anti-Catholicism here too, but the episode is mainly entertaining, and the paradox is an obvious one.

In all these episodes, then—the Macraeons, Quaresmeprenant, the Papimanes, the Papefigues, and Gaster—there is no action, and paradox or ambiguity is not the main point. Quaresmeprenant and Gaster are visually grotesque, Homenaz morally so, as is shown by his complacent refrains. And none of these people advance the quest in the slightest, not even the Macrobe, who might have been the ideal counselor.

All the other episodes in the book are based on the kind of paradox about language which we have discussed in the case of Medamothi, the storm, and the *alliances*. The most obvious of these is chapter 17. The expression "nous ne trouvasmes que frire" (i.e., "nothing," once again) suggests to Rabelais that there is literally nothing to fry with because Bringuenarilles has eaten all the cooking utensils, and the death of Bringuenarilles leads him into an erudite enumeration of unusual deaths quoted from various Classical and modern authors.

Once again a figurative expression taken literally has created an entire episode.

The most interesting episode in the book, from the point of view of Rabelais's creative technique, is the battle with the Andouilles (chs. 35–42). This is also in theory an episode of action, but most of the many pretexts on which it is based are linguistic. Rabelais may well have started from the name Rifl'Andouille, which he had already used in *Pantagruel* (ch. 29) and which he took from a medieval *mystère* or from a sermon by Michel Menot.[52] What better joke than to provide real *andouilles* to justify his name and to give him a colleague called Tailleboudin (ch. 37)? Now there is no doubt about which human member is evoked by a *boudin,* so Rabelais takes the joke one step further by providing the Andouilles (feminine in gender) with a queen (feminine) called Niphleseth ("penis" in Hebrew).

But this is just one possibility suggested by *andouilles.* There is also the expression "rompre les andouilles au genoil" (ch. 41, "to attempt something quite impractical"), which Pantagruel does literally during the battle, and the street in Paris called "la rue Pavée d'Andouilles," for which an explanation is here provided (the *andouilles* sent to Gargantua were given to the king, died, and were buried there). Other subsidiary jokes arise, like "cervelat ecervelé" (ch. 41).

The episode also balances the Quaresmeprenant description, since the *andouilles* are the natural enemies of Lent, and of course the entire action burlesques both the epic (the "grande Truye" is the Trojan horse, Gymnaste has a sword called "Baise mon cul") and the Grail quest ("moustarde estoit leur Sangreal et Bausme celeste"). Rabelais seldom found a subject which encouraged his verve to expand in so many different directions. In retrospect, the development of Bringuenarilles from "nous ne trouvasmes que frire" looks like a sketch for the much more complex use of language to create the Andouilles.

---

[52] See the critical edition, IV, 302, note 57; and *Sermons choisis de Michel Menot,* ed. Joseph Nève (Paris: Champion, 1924), p. 96: "Et esto quod ancilla sic faciat, non sequitur quod debeatis esse latro *et grosse rifle andoulle.*"

The island of Ruach (chs. 43–44) arose similarly from two expressions—the first metaphorical, "ils ne vivent que de vent" and the second literal, "petite pluie abat grand vent"—which had been used obscenely before Rabelais. The paradox seems particularly piquant in this case—living on wind is already sufficiently futile, and writing about wind is even more so. To call speech "wind" is pejorative, and writing is not so far removed from speech. Rabelais is at the same time laughing at the futility of writing at all and extracting, as is his custom, all the possible material from wind as a subject and as a pretext for verbal play (*vens couliz, ventoses, sonnets*). Might one not say, indeed, that all writers "ne vivent que de vent"?

The *parolles gelées* episode (chs. 55–56), which has provoked some critical argument, can be considered the other side of the question.[53] On the island of Ruach the insubstantial character of the writer's art was emphasized, but at the same time a positive side to this insubstantiality was suggested; *le vent* both represented nothingness and served as a starting point for positive verbal creation. This suggestion is carried further by the *parolles gelées:* literally, the raw material of the writer which he can use as he pleases for creation. Rabelais's whole work is full of his verbal exuberance, and here we have an allegory related to that exuberance: the words, any words, which are "frozen" until he cares to use them. It is just possible that the episode also refers, as Saulnier claims, to the necessity of hiding one's evangelical beliefs until the time is more appropriate for airing them. One of the attractions of this mysterious episode is that it could be an allegory of so many things, but given Rabelais's constant preoccupation with words and their use, the one I have suggested appears very likely. Moreover, in chapter 56, as well as a play on "motz de gueule," there is a brief discussion on *parolles* and their use. Panurge asks for some more

[53] See particularly Saulnier, "Le silence de Rabelais et le mythe des paroles gelées," in *François Rabelais,* pp. 233–47, who sees historical references; and Jean Guiton, "Le mythe des paroles gelées," *RR* XXXI (1940), 3–15, and Spitzer, "Rabelais et les rabelaisants," who interpret the myth as an allusion to Rabelais's own creative methods. This is also the view of David Kuhn, *La poétique de François Villon* (Paris: Colin, 1967), pp. 279–80, and of Jean Paris.

frozen words, and Pantagruel replies "que donner parolles estoit acte des amoureux." Panurge then asks him to sell them, and his answer is "C'est acte de advocatz vendre parolles. Je vous vendroys plus tost silence." This conversation can be taken simply as a joke or as a serious statement about the way words should be used. The whole episode is the culmination of Rabelais's preoccupation with words in this book; for Bringuenarilles, the *alliances,* and the Andouilles he takes metaphorical expressions literally and gives them a concrete reality; here he gives this reality to the words themselves. This episode alone is sufficient to show the superficiality of critical judgments like Tetel's: "Il faut distinguer entre le comique que le langage exprime et celui que le langage crée." [54] Rabelais's genius lies precisely in fusing them, in using the one in the service of the other.

Chapter 63 has often been praised as a remarkable, and unusual, picture of people doing nothing during a calm at sea. It has not been noticed, however, that these three chapters (63–65) are based on exactly the same technique as the ones we have just discussed: the literal presentation of a figurative expression, in this case "haulser le temps." There is some action/language paradox here too; the characters are only chatting so entertainingly because they are unable to act, and the result of taking "haulser le temps" literally is that the weather, in this case the wind, does "get up," so that the action can continue.

This passage would have made a very satisfactory ending for the *Quart livre,* and it is just like Rabelais to end with chapters 66–67, which pose all sorts of problems. Is this simply another indecisive ending like the ambiguous enigma of *Gargantua?* It would not be surprising for Panurge's quest to come to an end with no proper conclusion, particularly if Rabelais intended to conclude it in the next book. But Saulnier has evolved a disquieting theory which would give the ending a very different flavor.[55] According to him, chapter 66 contains

[54] Tetel, *Etude sur le comique de Rabelais,* p. 81.
[55] V.-L. Saulnier, "Pantagruel au large de Ganabin ou la peur de Panurge," *BHR* XVI (1954), 58–81.

detailed references to the forces of repression and injustice, in particular to the prisons of Paris. The attitudes of the three main characters are opposed, as usual; Panurge is terrified, Frere Jean wants to attack, which would be foolish and disastrous, while the wise Pantagruel simply refuses to land. This ties up very well with Saulnier's basic view of Rabelais and would provide a neat conclusion. In any case, the final chapter is as facetious as possible and would provide an excellent contrast to the basically serious preceding chapter.

As in the *Tiers livre,* Rabelais has by no means abandoned his earlier comic effects. The giant theme reappears briefly during the storm, when Pantagruel holds the mast to keep it from breaking (ch. 19). The Dindenault bargaining scene is an excellent example of Panurge's expenditure of time and energy for petty revenge. Chronology is seldom in question, but the chatty interlude during the storm (long discussion about wills in ch. 21) and the battle with the Andouilles (learned disquisition on names in ch. 37) hold up the action long enough to destroy any possibility of *vraisemblance.* And there is no shortage of pithy jokes and stories and verbal humor. In fact, the general tone is definitely more lighthearted than in the *Tiers livre,* and the maximum entertainment value is extracted from each grotesque encounter.

But our preceding analysis of episodes shows that the *Quart livre* is just as fundamentally paradoxical and disconcerting as the *Tiers livre.* Its twenty episodes are as diverse as possible: overt satire (the Papimanes), grotesque pictures with some moral import (Quaresmeprenant and Gaster), apparently straightforward action (the storm, the whale, and the Andouilles), apparently straightforward anecdote (the Chiquanous and the Papefigues), a humanist profession of faith (the Macraeons). Of these twenty episodes, seven—Medamothi, the *alliances,* Bringuenarilles, the Andouilles, Ruach, the *parolles gelées,* and "haulser le temps"—are based entirely on words or idiomatic expressions. So the book is a false epic in two ways: first, the impression of action is illusory, since nothing actually happens; second, incident is created, lit-

erally, out of words. The *Tiers livre* was obviously a book about words; the *Quart livre* is, in fact, a book about words while pretending to be an action-packed epic quest. This is not only excellent bluff on the literary level but it also raises doubts in our minds about the relative natures of action and words in human life.

CONCLUSION

Let us take one last look at our contemporary reader, who by this time must be beyond surprise. He has been given, in order, a false successor to the *Grandes Chronicques* which combines satire and enigma to attack a disconcertingly varied selection of targets; a false successor to *Pantagruel* which is chronologically a predecessor and a quite different kind of book, positive where *Pantagruel* was negative; a false continuation of *Gargantua* which is really a continuation of *Pantagruel,* where nothing happens at all and where the inquiry about marriage turns out to be a pseudo-inquiry having almost nothing to do with marriage; and finally a false continuation of the *Tiers livre* in which apparent action turns out to be language. If we were to ask him what kind of book the work as a whole is, he would have no answer. It is not "about" any one thing, it does not have "a" major character, and any description of it would have to take a leaf from Polonius's book. A fictional-topical-polemical-educational-comical prose work, perhaps?

This lack of any unifying thread is just one of the disconcerting aspects which have been recognized and enjoyed by generations of readers. The very richness of the book is itself disconcerting: the energy and gusto with which Rabelais describes, satirizes, or demolishes any subject under the sun. Like the intellectual dialogues discussed in Chapter I, the four books are a compendium of what the sixteenth century knew and thought about science, medicine, geography, philosophy, botany, architecture, education, kingship, etymology, warfare, navigation, costume, heraldry, evangelism, divination, marriage, jurisprudence, gastronomy, viticulture, and meteorology. Each chapter is an autonomous unit, to be appreciated on its own terms rather than in terms of the work as a whole.

In many cases Rabelais gives us the exact opposite of what we are expecting, in the domain of subject or of tone. The most frequent of these straightforward oppositions are: comedy/seriousness, action/language, clarity/obscurity, brevity/long-windedness, and fantasy/*vraisemblance*. But what I have tried to show in this chapter is that obvious antitheses like these are just the beginning of Rabelais's techniques of shock. We have examined cases where the comic/serious dichotomy, for instance, will not work, and others where Rabelais is playing with the whole concept of *vraisemblance*. And we have seen that just about every aspect of the work can be disconcerting. Whole books are not what they seem, characters change, unlikely episodes and contrasting styles follow each other, chapters begin in one vein and end in another, words shift their connotations in mid-sentence, enigmas turn out to be *coqs-à-l'âne,* staggering inventiveness is devoted to trivial or nonexistent pretexts while apparently serious matters are dismissed in a few words. When ambiguity is itself in question, it is seldom straightforward; not only are things not as they appear to be, but we never do find out how they really are. Each book apparently ends with a great big question mark.

What, then, can we be sure of? In the present state of acrimonious critical disagreement it would seem that we can be sure of nothing except that a lot of Rabelais is very funny. It is no longer possible even to attempt to reconcile the opposing critical views and methodologies, so I can only state my own position. I agree with Screech that we can be sure of a few things: Rabelais is supporting an Erasmian stand on religious issues; some passages in the work are intended to be taken seriously, and one way to identify these is that when Rabelais is serious, he is brief; all of Rabelais's references to the subjects enumerated above must be read with an eye on the intellectual background with which he is identifying. I am also convinced, and although I cannot prove it conclusively, I have tried in this chapter to present the evidence in favor of it, that we can be sure of one more thing. Rabelais's interest in, and use of, shock techniques or bluff are central to his work and give a kind of unity—though not, of course, in the Classical sense—to a book which has no other conceivable kind of unity. I am not, by saying this, falling into the "tidying up" trap which I deplored at the beginning of my first chapter. I am, essentially, advocating a state of mind in the reader —anticipation of the unexpected—which will enable him to appreciate as fully as a modern reader can the richness and complexity of Rabelais.

I have also tried to show that bluff, as well as being present in many forms throughout the work, develops significantly from book to book. In *Pantagruel,* the lightheartedly destructive first book, it is fairly easy to separate the bluff from the serious. The enigmas and the ambiguities, though they may have a serious satiric purpose, are essentially intellectual parlor games intended to amuse and intrigue the reader. In the much more real, moral, and constructive *Gargantua* ambiguity is more fundamental and bluff often becomes double bluff. Episodes like the "Propos des bien yvres" and the Picrocholine war can be interpreted on several levels at once. Verisimilitude is played with to blur the distinction between the worlds of reality and fantasy, ambiguous themes become more important, and paradox becomes subtler and at the same time more persuasive. Between this book and the next Rabelais's attitude would appear to have changed radically, for the *Tiers livre* is to a large extent *about* ambiguity—its causes, manifestations, and effects. This intellectual attitude does not replace the earlier, more playful attitude but supplements it, so that one might subtitle this book *Theory and Practice of Bluff.* And the *Quart livre,* of whose overall intent I am much less sure, provides a fascinating exercise in bluff on the fictional level, in its creation of "action" episodes out of nothing or out of words. This development from book to book shows that Rabelais not only remained interested in the techniques which create bluff, he became more and more interested in the whole subject of paradox and ambiguity and how they function.

I stated at the beginning of this chapter that I would not attempt any classification of Rabelais's shock techniques. I have attempted to give as many examples as possible of what seem to me the most important ones, to discuss in some detail points which have been overlooked by previous critics, and to trace an obvious evolution in Rabelais's attitude toward paradox and ambiguity. My main aim is a modest one: to demonstrate that if, as I have tried to show, Rabelais's primary purpose was to disconcert his reader, then he has amply succeeded.

CHAPTER III

Montaigne and
the Art of Bluff

"C'est icy un livre de bonne foy, lecteur," says Montaigne, and for four centuries this statement has been generally accepted at face value.[1] Florio, however, translated it as "a well-meaning book,"[2] which has a certain tongue-in-cheek flavor, and my main thesis in this chapter will be that Montaigne and his book are very seldom *de bonne foy*, so that taking either of them at face value is hazardous, to say the least. I do not mean simply that many of Montaigne's statements are not true; this has long been admitted and is, in any case, only one aspect of the matter. I mean that the book, and Montaigne as presented in the book, are essentially illustrations of the art of bluff. This is composed of deliberate untruth, ambiguity, irony, paradox, and contradiction, out of which diverse elements Montaigne has created a unified work of art.

Montaigne criticism is vast and varied, but two basic assumptions are common to nearly all of it: first, that Montaigne is fundamentally a moralist and his book "un manuel de sagesse,"[3] and second, that his

[1] All references are to *Les essais de Michel de Montaigne, édition . . . Pierre Villey, réimprimée . . . V.-L. Saulnier* (Paris: P.U.F., 1965). References will usually be incorporated in the text, with page numbers.

[2] *Selected Essays of Montaigne in the Translation of John Florio,* ed. Walter Kaiser (Boston: Riverside Press, 1964), p. 2.

[3] See Armaingaud, in his 1924 edition of the *Essais,* among many others.

main intention in the *Essais* is to paint a portrait of himself. I should like to challenge the "fundamentally" and the "main" in these assumptions and to examine the evidence which points to a very different Montaigne: fundamentally an astute and humorous intellectual, whose main intention is to jolt, disconcert, and amuse his reader. Of course, "Montaigne moraliste," in the broad sense defined by Hugo Friedrich, exists; the essays are full of wisdom and common sense and will continue to be read for that reason among others.[4] There is likewise a great deal of wisdom in Shakespeare, some of it borrowed from Montaigne, but nobody to my knowledge ever called *King Lear* a *manuel de sagesse*. "Montaigne peintre de lui-même" also exists and will continue to fascinate critics by his description of thought describing itself thinking.[5] Montaigne talks about himself for many reasons, one of which is that by criticizing himself, he can indirectly and without offense criticize his contemporaries, as I shall discuss later. Any writer who constantly talks about himself is necessarily creating a self-portrait. My point here is simply this: I would not deny for a moment the value of Montaigne's moral viewpoint or the interest and charm of his self-portrait. What I would maintain is that too much attention has been given to these two aspects and not nearly enough to what seems to me the heart of the matter: Montaigne the creator and user of paradox, ambiguity, and *boutade*.

In order to present as clearly as possible the evidence in favor of my view of Montaigne, I shall first discuss in general what seem to me his basic preoccupations and then analyze in some detail a few essays from each of his three books, to explore his use of these preoccupations. This chronological treatment may seem arbitrary, but as in the case of Rabelais, I think it is justified. Montaigne did not write the essays in the order in which we have them, but he did choose to pre-

---

[4] Hugo Friedrich, *Montaigne*, tr. Robert Rovini (Paris: Gallimard, 1968), especially pp. 189 ff.

[5] There are excellent discussions, leading to varied conclusions, in Friedrich, *Montaigne*; Philip Hallie, *The Scar of Montaigne* (Middletown, Conn.: Wesleyan University Press, 1966); R. A. Sayce, "Montaigne et la peinture du passage," *SRLF* IV (1963), 11–59; and Michael Baraz, *L'être et la connaissance selon Montaigne* (Paris: Corti, 1968).

sent them to the reader in this order. Sometimes it is not clear why, but some essays do hang together in groups by subject matter. Moreover, much harm has been done to Montaigne by the critical habit of collecting all his statements on a given topic and discussing them all together; this procedure is sometimes necessary, but surely the best way to approach a writer is to consider his work as an artistic unit, and each essay is such a unit. Many men have shared Montaigne's ideas, but very few have made literature out of them.

BASIC PREOCCUPATIONS

Montaigne, like many educated people of his time and ours, has three main concerns, one moral, one intellectual, and one artistic. On the moral plane he is interested in the nature of man and life, the definition of virtue and courage, the moral aspects of war and education. In moral matters his philosophy tends toward stoicism, in the sense of acceptance of life's problems and refusal to indulge in metaphysical speculation. His moral concerns are those of all men, but he is particularly interested in such problems of his time as torture, sorcery, and the wars of religion. However, his moral attitude has been consistently misunderstood, even by those critics who have made it their main concern, and here we must return for a moment to the question of *bonne foy*. Certainly Montaigne says, "Je n'enseigne poinct, je raconte" (III, ii, 806) and "Je ne me mesle pas de dire ce qu'il faut faire au monde" (I, xxviii, 192), and states repeatedly that he is talking about himself, not the world ("Je n'ay affaire qu'à moy," III, xvii, 657). Before accepting these statements at their face value, let us examine the essays to see if they agree with the statements. W will find, of course, that they do not. Try counting the number of times Montaigne uses *il faut* and imperative expressions—"il faut oster le masque aussi bien des choses, que des personnes" (I, xx, 96), for instance, is nothing if not a moral imperative. Consider the number of contemporary problems on which

Montaigne gives sound moral advice: religious differences of opinion (I, xxiii), military strategy (I, v), diplomatic procedure (I, xvii), education (I, xxv and xxvi), the French legal system (III, xiii), judicial torture (II, xxvii), the treatment of sorcerers (III, xi), the behavior of colonists (I, xxxi), conduct in public office (III, x), the regulation of extravagance in dress (I, xliii), the right use of money (I, xiv), the true role of woman (III, ix), and many more. It is quite possible to see Book I as a manual of behavior for the *gentilhomme,* as does Butor, and the whole book provides a comprehensive survey of the problems of the time, in which Montaigne's own moral attitude is never in doubt.[6] All this makes nonsense of *je n'enseigne poinct,* and in any case, *je n'enseigne poinct, je raconte* is a false antithesis. A great many of Montaigne's *contes* have a moral *enseignement,* like the *exempla* in sermons. Moreover, Montaigne uses himself as a cover for moral judgments—he often seems to be chastizing himself when, in fact, he is castigating humanity, so that "tout homme porte la forme entiere de l'humaine condition" is double-edged. It is a reassuring call to solidarity, a consolation to the obscure and lonely, but it is also a reproach to other men who do not come to the same ethical conclusions as Montaigne.

On the moral plane, then, Montaigne is already using bluff like the sugar coating on the pill, to state a firm moral viewpoint without appearing to do so. On all the moral issues mentioned he is quite sure where he stands, and there is no question of suspension of judgment. His constant self-denigration, to which we shall return, has a sound moral pretext—if we are led to sympathize with him, we shall be more likely to accept his moral outlook. Ambiguity arises only when we fail to distinguish between his attitude to the problem discussed, which is invariably quite straightforward, and his attitude to the reader, which is often falsely humble and self-deprecating. He often, in fact, deliberately deceives the reader rather than merely disconcerts him.

6 Michel Butor, *Essais sur les Essais* (Paris: Gallimard, 1968).

On the intellectual plane the situation is more complex. Like Rabelais, Montaigne's main concern is destructive. He sets out to show us that our thought processes are rudimentary and superficial, that "nous ne goustons rien de pur," that what we call *gloire* or *repentir* is, in fact, no such matter, and that there are far more sides to every argument than we think. He employs every possible kind of contradiction, antithesis, and paradox to shake the reader out of his intellectual complacency, but he does it, as we shall see, in a far subtler manner than Rabelais—so subtle, indeed, that generations of readers have missed most of the point altogether.

If Montaigne can be called a stoic on moral issues, intellectually he is a skeptic, too convinced of the fallibility of human judgment (always excepting his own) to rely on it. And neither his moral nor his intellectual outlook changes in the course of the book. His main intellectual preoccupation was and remained diversity, as the title of the first essay indicates. He was eternally fascinated by the inability of the human mind to move in a straight line. The titles of the essays can be divided into what we think about (*oisiveté, moderation, présomption*) and how we think ("Que nos affections s'emportent au delà de nous"). In the first case the paradox is basically in Montaigne's treatment of a subject the reader had accepted without question, whereas in the second group the emphasis is on the paradox of the reader's thought processes, which Montaigne analyzes objectively. In this group the title often contains the judgment Montaigne intends us to make on the subject: "Qu'il ne fault juger de nostre heur qu'apres la mort" or "L'heure des parlemens dangereuse." Or the title contains a paradox: "Comme nous pleurons et rions d'une mesme chose," or "Des mauvais moyens employez à bonne fin," or "Que philosopher, c'est apprendre à mourir." So we are not altogether surprised to find that where the title appears more straightforward, it is actually even less so. "La fortune se rencontre souvent au train de la raison" turns out to be a paradox—we would logically expect the opposite to be the case. "De la parsimonie des anciens" is a condemnation of the lack of *parsimonie* of the moderns, and "De la force de l'imagination" mainly concerns the bad or irrelevant aspects of this *force*.

These last titles are already in the first group mentioned, in which Montaigne applies his own intellect to demolishing our preconceived ideas on many different subjects, most of them in the domain of ethics, to showing that there is a positive as well as a negative aspect to some vices (I, ix); that a word like *gloire* is simply a word and corresponds to no reality (II, xvi); or that what we call *amitié* should be called something else (I, xxviii). A large proportion of essays have abstract titles (for instance, I, ii, viii, xii, xviii, xxviii, xxx, xxxix; II, v, xi, xvi, xvii, xxvii, xxix; III, ii, ix, xiii), and in each case Montaigne shows that the concept in question is so complex that the name is positively misleading. One of the best examples of this is "De l'utile et de l'honneste," in which Montaigne's conclusion will be not simply that *l'utile* and *l'honneste* are irreconcilable but that the standard opposition between them is a false one, and that the two words belong to quite different, and not necessarily opposed, frames of reference.

Many titles in both groups, then, indicate an intellectual interest in paradox. Many other titles, particularly in the subjects-we-think-about group, are deliberately misleading. In "Des cannibales" the concept to be demolished is that of *barbare,* the subject of II, iii, is death and that of III, xi, is sorcery. The titles "Sur des vers de Virgile," "Coutume de l'isle de Cea," and "L'histoire de Spurina" look like introductions to guessing games; how quickly will the reader realize that the subjects being treated are, respectively, sex, suicide, and chastity?

It has often been said that Montaigne's title gives little indication of what the essay is about. Inasmuch as most essays are about several different things, this is true; what the titles do indicate very clearly is Montaigne's wish to disconcert or mislead his reader. After a while the reader accepts this as natural and expects to be told that "la cruauté" is far more complex and far-reaching than he had thought (II, xi) or that "la ressemblance des enfans aux peres" (II, xxxvii) can inspire reflections on subjects as varied and general as medicine, old age, pain, presumption, experience, diversity, and heredity. The titles are the reader's first indication that paradox may be Montaigne's main intellectual preoccupation; the second indication is the frequency, in the first few sentences of each essay, of words expressing contradiction or diversity. In Book I there are only nine essays which do not contain, in the first three sentences, one of the following words: *mais* or *ains* (in 23 cases, plus a *mais* in sentence 4 of I, xxv), *toutesfois* (3), *si est-ce que* (1), *au rebours* (3), *ou bien* or *ou* meaning "on the other hand" (2), *divers* or *diversité* (6), *erreur* (1), *difference* (1), *estrangeté* (1), *inconnuës* (1), *distance* (1), *contraire* (2 in French, 1 in Latin), *et pour et contre* in French and Greek (1). Of the nine exceptions, I, xiii, begins with a *boutade:* "Il n'est subject si vain qui ne merite un rang en cette rapsodie," and I, xv, with a paradox: "La vaillance a ses limites, comme les autres vertus." The title of I, xxii, is a paradox, if a banal one; I, xxx, begins with a paradox on virtue similar to that of I, xv; I, xlviii, with a lighthearted and quite untrue disclaimer to any knowledge of grammar; I, xli, and I, l, have a paradox in the third sentence (the third *a* sentence in I, xli); and I, lvii, has a *si* meaning "however" in sentence 4. Of 57 essays, only 3 (I, xxx, xxxv, and lii) do not open on a note of paradox, contradiction, or playfulness. In Book II, of 37 essays, only ix, x, and xxiv do not so begin, and in Book III, of 13, only i.

This is already impressive evidence of an overriding preoccupation. A man who so often uses *mais* and *au contraire* is a man accustomed to seeing both, or all, sides of a question, who will exploit all the possibilities of existing paradoxes and then go on to create new ones. It is certainly true that this delight in paradox can already be found in the works of compilation which influenced Montaigne's development as a writer, but as we shall see when we come to analyze individual essays,

Montaigne's additions to his sources, as well as his own additions to the earliest form of an essay, frequently add to or enlarge upon the original paradox.

In the first two domains we are considering, then, we can already see Montaigne's tendency to work on several levels at once. His moral attitude is basically firm and serious, though his attitude to the reader is falsely deprecating, and his intellectual attitude always tends toward paradox and *boutade*. In an essay on, say, repentance (III, ii) it will not be easy to distinguish these two attitudes or to discern at what point he shifts from serious-moral to intellectual-playful in tone. This problem is further compounded by consideration of his third main interest, the artistic.

It is quite possible to form a reasonably clear idea of "what Montaigne is like" morally and intellectually, though I admit that critics are far from agreement on the subject. But there is at least a great deal of evidence in the essays from which to argue. It is rather surprising that there is so little evidence of his artistic taste in most domains. He seems, indeed, to have very little of what we call "taste." In the *Journal de voyage* he is much less interested in art and architecture than in people and customs, and he appears to choose his reading on moral and intellectual, rather than aesthetic, grounds (although he does have some taste for poetry). The only artistic subject in which we know he was interested is the structure and style of his own essays. We can therefore compare what he says he is doing with what he is doing, and, of course, we find another complete contradiction. On moral matters he pretends to be remote and unconcerned while, in fact, giving sound and firm judgment; when talking about the essays, he pretends to be an amateur writer with a clumsy style and no internal structure, while the essays themselves clearly demonstrate the opposite.[7] There is no doubt

---

[7] Cf. Floyd Gray, *Le style de Montaigne* (Paris: Nizet, 1958), and the articles by Baraz and Starobinski quoted in note 22; Morris Parslow, "Montaigne's Composition: A Study of the Structure of the Essays of the Third Book" (Ph.D. diss., Princeton University, 1954); and Wolf E. Traeger, *Aufbau und Gedankenführung in Montaignes Essais* (Heidelberg: C. Winter, 1961).

at all that the aesthetic aspect of the *Essais* is extremely important for him, that his writing is self-conscious, that each essay has an internal structure, and that his varied use of additions has its reasons.

We have already seen, then, that in each of these three areas of preoccupation—the moral, the intellectual, and the artistic—paradox and ambiguity are present. And it is obvious that in most essays the three areas will overlap. The tidiest way of putting this is to say that intellect is used to analyze moral issues, and art to express the analysis, and this seems to be the general critical approach. (There are honorable exceptions to this rule, which I shall mention in due course.) But Montaigne, as a man of his time, consistently sees any one of these preoccupations in terms of the other two, and this is the first level on which bluff operates in the *Essais*.

For instance, the gulf between appearance and reality is essentially a moral problem and can, indeed, have serious moral consequences, like encouraging people to be "plus desireux de grande que de bonne reputation" (II, xvi, 626), so that virtue is subordinated to popularity. In this case the distinction between appearance and reality is bad, but in other cases it is good: "Le Maire et Montaigne ont tousjours esté deux, d'une separation bien claire," because "il faut jouer deuement nostre rolle, mais comme rolle d'un personnage emprunté. Du masque et de l'apparence il n'en faut pas faire une essence réelle" (III, x, 1012 and 1011). This is the moral aspect (double, as usual), but Montaigne is attracted at the same time by the intellectual aspect (the weak thought processes which fail to distinguish between the mask and the man) and by the artistic, in this case theatrical, aspect of the man, his mask, and his role. So we have three attitudes, apparently mutually exclusive, operating at once: morally he will express a firm judgment (it is immoral to reject reality for appearance); intellectually he will analyze the clumsy reasoning in question; and aesthetically he will record with pleasure any artistic symmetry or theatrical paradox.

This multilevel approach to an issue is exemplified by Montaigne's use of the key themes in the *Essais*. For example, one would expect *la présomption* to be essentially a moral question, but Montaigne seems mainly interested, especially in the "Apologie," in the intellectual steps which produce it, and his aim in that essay is to destroy *intellectually* a *moral* attitude. Presumption also produces aesthetically entertaining situations, like that of Xerxes whipping the Hellespont (I, iv, 23).

An even better example of such a theme is *la diversité*. Its basic attraction is artistic and already paradoxical: diversity of custom, dress, religion, and so on at first appears negative, since the opposing points of view cancel each other out. But further exploration reveals a pattern in diversity, and Montaigne loves a pattern in any domain, as we shall see. Diversity is also intellectual, in that it illustrates the incredibly varied workings of the human mind, and observation of diversity can lead to a moral attitude of tolerance and mutual forbearance.

So this interaction of the three domains we have been discussing is bound to create ambiguity and a constant shift of viewpoint, which, added to Montaigne's paradoxical attitude on moral and artistic questions, goes a good way toward disconcerting the reader. In "Des menteurs," which I shall analyze in detail later on, all three considerations are simultaneously present: on the moral plane his poor memory guarantees him from the vices of lying and ambition, intellectually it has various advantages and disadvantages, and aesthetically it enables him to reread books with the same pleasure. Here each domain is separate, but in the "Apologie" they are mingled, with a certain amount of *mauvaise foi:* Montaigne is at the same time condemning human reason for its constant fluctuation and taking artistic pleasure in the spectacle of this fluctuation.

The main themes of the *Essais* are those in which Montaigne is interested from all three points of view: *diversité, coutume, présomption, inegalité, incertitude.* Besides these themes there are three all-important subjects to be considered in this connection: Montaigne's self-portrait, the essays themselves, and *la parole.* I shall take the last first because it is closer to the themes we have just been discussing and because it is the one major preoccupation which Montaigne shares with

Rabelais.[8] I shall analyze later several passages which are devoted almost entirely to this subject; let me simply underline at this point the importance of *la parole* in the *Essais,* as it has been very little discussed.

On the moral plane *la parole,* in the sense of "word of honor," is so important for Montaigne that he devotes to it the major part of six essays: "Si le chef d'une place assiégée doit sortir pour parlementer" (I, v), "L'heure des parlemens dangereuse" (I, vi), "Que l'intention juge nos actions" (I, vii), "Du démentir" (II, xviii), "De la colere" (II, xxxi), and "De l'utile et de l'honneste" (III, i). Many more essays emphasize the intellectual importance of words. They can be misused by liars (I, ix), but this is hazardous and not always successful; different ways of speaking are useful in different circumstances ("Du parler prompt ou tardif," I, x); words pronounced by authority, especially if obscure, can have a mysterious and quite unjustified power ("Des prognostications," I, xi); the right use and understanding of words and the distinction between "faits" and "paroles" are essential to education (I, xxv and xxvi); names very often have no connection with things and, anyway, have no intrinsic value (I, xlvi); in fact, we should all be aware of "la vanité des paroles" (I, li); the word *gloire,* for instance, corresponds to no absolute reality (II, xvi); in anger, as in other domains, "le dire est autre chose que le faire" (II, xxxi); conversation is the best form of communication (III, iii); and it is essential to know how to organize words properly when conducting a formal argument (III, viii).

In all these essays the use or misuse of words is the essential point. In just about every essay the word *parole* occurs in an enormous variety of contexts and a mixture of moral and intellectual discussions. Words must be rightly used in prayer (I, lvi), and the Protestants are wrong to think that the Word of God can be interpreted by any "garçon de boutique." Law, like scholarship, suffers from an overdose of words—"nous ne faisons que nous entregloser" (III, xiii). Our grief

---

[8] See my article, "Rabelais and the Comedy of the Spoken Word," *MLR* LXIII (1968), 575–80.

is frequently "une plainte grammairienne et voyelle" (III, iv), and our whole attitude to sex is bound up with "superstition verbale" (III, v). Book III, essay viii, is almost entirely about language. The gap between words and what they are supposed to convey fascinates Montaigne as it did Rabelais, though here again Montaigne's approach is often more subtle.

What Montaigne has to say about his own use of words has often been discussed, and here again there is a complete contradiction between what he does and what he says he does. "Le parler que j'ayme, c'est un parler simple et naif, tel sur le papier qu'à la bouche" (I, xxvi, 171); "je n'ay ny composition, ny explication qui vaille" (I, xxi, 106); "[mon langage] est aspre et desdaigneux" (II, xvii, 638)—of these and other similar statements there are three possible interpretations. (1) Montaigne believes exactly what he says, and it's true (Friedrich); (2) Montaigne believes exactly what he says because he is not aware that his style is very different from this (Thibaudet, Gray); and (3) Montaigne is perfectly well aware that his style is not like this, and he is indulging in deliberate self-deprecation (Baraz, Parslow, Traeger). The last interpretation seems to me the only possible one; Montaigne's style is much too well balanced, too intellectual, and too metaphorical to be unconscious, and his devaluation of it is analogous to his pretense of lack of moral commitment. A man who writes spontaneously, as he speaks, will be more endearing to the reader than a self-conscious rhetorician, so Montaigne will pretend to be that man. I do not, however, agree with Baraz that the purpose of this self-deprecation is exclusively serious.

La parole as a theme underlies all the essays and serves to show up paradoxes on the moral and intellectual planes; it is used for deliberate bluff by Montaigne on the artistic plane. The same applies to the self-portrait theme, perhaps the most-discussed aspect of Montaigne. Here there are two main interpretations: (1) Montaigne is genuinely trying to paint a complete and "sincere" portrait of himself (nearly all critics); (2) Montaigne is painting a literary portrait which is not intended to be taken at face value (Baraz, Bowen, and, interestingly enough, Strowski).[9] Let us examine some of the evidence for this view.

We know, to begin with, that many of Montaigne's statements, if taken at face value, are simply not true. "Je propose une vie basse et sans lustre" (III, ii, 805) is nonsense if taken literally (of course, both *Je* and *propose* are deliberately ambiguous). We know that he played a political role and was an acquaintance, if not a friend, of two kings, and his "Je n'ay eu guere en maniement que mes affaires" (II, xvii, 643) is contradicted by "En ce peu que j'ay eu à negotier entre nos Princes" (III, i, 791) and by "l'accez que fortune m'a donné aux chefs de divers partis" (I, xxi, 106).[10] We know that he exaggerates the aristocracy of his family and his own part in certain military exploits,[11] and it is possible that his story of how his courage disarmed brigands is not true (III, xii, 1061–62).[12] As Professor Gray says himself, "Ne soyons pas trop crédules."[13] Similar exaggerations are frequent in connection with his character—"Tout est grossier chez moi"—and intellect —"J'ay l'esprit tardif et mousse" (II, xvii, 637, 651) or "l'apprehension molle et lâche" (I, xxxix, 242)—and it seems unlikely, to say the least, that his memory is as bad as he says it is. Neither are "je n'entens rien au Grec" (II, iv, 363) or "[je] ne scay encore que c'est d'adjectif, conjunctif et d'ablatif" (I, xlviii, 287) to be taken literally. All these statements, in fact, are of the same type as the denigrations of his style already noted; they give us a picture of an endearingly ordinary, run-of-the-mill fellow, a little thick-headed, with no pretensions to wit or elegance but full of good intentions. The picture is charming, but there is plenty of external and internal evidence for a very different Montaigne: a man of considerable public importance, mayor of Bordeaux,

---

[9] See Fortunat Strowski, *Montaigne,* 2nd ed. (Paris: Alcan, 1931), ch. VII and especially p. 328.

[10] For biographical details, see Donald Frame, *Montaigne, a Biography* (New York: Harcourt, Brace, and World, 1965).

[11] See Paul Ballaguy, "La sincérité de Montaigne," *Mercure de France* (July–Aug. 1933), pp. 547–75.

[12] See Ballaguy, "La sincérité de Montaigne"; Gray, *Le style,* p. 248; and Frame's review of Gray's book in *RR* L (1959), 209–11.

[13] Gray, *Le style,* p. 247.

negotiator between the king and Henri de Navarre, friendly with princes, diplomats, and humanists, conversant with a great deal of Classical literature, and, as we have noted, more than willing to give moral advice to his readers.

Why, then, the devalued portrait? Friedrich considers the devaluation of himself and his book to be basically an amusing use of the literary *topos* of affected humility, with moralizing overtones of "my humility demonstrates my uniqueness." [14] Baraz regards it as an example of Socratic irony with fundamentally serious purpose: oblique moral instruction, so to speak, by presenting apparently "low" things in a favorable light. Certainly there is a distinct resemblance between Socrates on Socrates, Montaigne on Socrates, and Montaigne on Montaigne. Montaigne's description of the ideal youth in "De l'institution des enfants" is very similar to his description of Socrates in "De la phisionomie," and many critics have noted that Socrates was Montaigne's personal ideal.[15] Montaigne gives this impression himself, except in one passage where he disapproves of Socrates' "ecstases" (III, xiii, 1115). More important than the personal question, however, is the Silenus theme, which was very popular in Renaissance literature, as we saw in Chapter I.[16] Erasmus applies the Silenus image to Christ, perhaps the most extreme example of Socratic irony in the Renaissance. Baraz may be right in saying that Montaigne's self-deprecation has a serious moral purpose; even if it does, this does not mean that on the intellectual level he is not simply playing a game of bluff with the reader.

There is, in any case, a striking similarity between Montaigne's deprecation of himself and his deprecation of his book, and this raises the whole question of the "livre consubstantiel à son autheur" (II, xviii, 665). This statement has always been taken quite seriously, which I

---

[14] Friedrich, *Montaigne*, p. 27.

[15] See, for instance, Frederick Kellerman, "The *Essais* and Socrates," *Symposium* X (1956), 204–16. See also Friedrich, Thibaudet, and many others.

[16] See p. 13 and note 14 of Chapter I. Baraz discusses this briefly in his book, Part III, ch. 2.

find surprising. Words in the sixteenth century are much closer to their etymological origins than they are today, and *consubstantiel à* means "being of one substance with." Luther apparently believed that the substance of the body and blood of Christ was present in the Eucharist *together with* (*cum*) the substance of bread and wine. The substance of a man is flesh and blood, and the substance of a book (in the philosophical sense) is words—and we know what Montaigne thinks about words. A child can be consubstantial with his father (and Montaigne specifically makes the analogy between children and essays in II, viii, 400–402), but a man cannot be consubstantial with a book. Certainly Montaigne may be creating a metaphor here, as he does elsewhere with *fricassée* and *bigarrure,* but even so I see no reason to suppose that he is making a serious statement, particularly since the prevailing tone of this essay is definitely lighthearted. The title is "Du dementir," but when Montaigne finally gets around to the subject, in the last paragraph (p. 667), he dismisses it again immediately: "Quant aux divers usages de nos démentirs, et les loix de nostre honneur en cela, et les changemens qu'elles ont receu, je remets à une autre-fois d'en dire ce que j'en sçay." At the beginning of the essay he produces the old *topos* of affected humility and actually quotes "Non recito cuiquam, nisi amicis," which is clearly a joke in the context. He has some very frivolous suggestions about possible practical uses for the *Essais* ("j'empescheray peut-estre que quelque coin de beurre ne se fonde au marché," p. 664), and even in the long interpolated passage which includes the "livre consubstantiel à son autheur" he is playing with ambiguity about himself and his book (see below, p. 147).

The remark, to my mind, is a *boutade,* and a rather daring one in view of the theological controversies of the time. Montaigne is perfectly well aware of the ambiguities inherent in all first-person narration, ambiguities which, ironically enough, have been thoroughly discussed apropos of Rousseau and Proust and hardly at all apropos of Montaigne. He emphasizes carefully and constantly the changeableness of his character and then contradicts himself with remarks about his "forme maistresse" (III, ii, 811). Moreover, this portrait of change is remarkably coherent, which may be why most of his critics claim to know him well, however much he claims that he doesn't know himself. He objects in "De l'inconstance de nos actions" to overhomogenized biographies (II, i, 332), but his self-portrait is, in fact, very consistent. The only subject on which he significantly changes his mind is death, and though he tells us he is always changing and fluctuating, there is very little internal evidence of this. The theme of universal change and flux, which goes back at least to Heraclitus, was one he found aesthetically attractive, as the concluding pages of the "Apologie" make clear, and the final impression we have of Montaigne is of a whole man whom we have come to know. This is a considerable tour de force— the constant emphasis on change, diversity, and unreliability has had the opposite effect to what was, apparently, intended. Is it not very probable that this exact effect was intended?

There is evidence for this conclusion in other remarks of Montaigne's about himself and his book. In the "Apologie" he states that his habit of upholding contrary opinions has been known to change his mind for him (II, xii, 566), which suggests an influence of his book upon his character. The analogy between himself and his book is, I suggest, an essentially literary device which helps to give unity to the *Essais*. No complete chapter is devoted to the essays, although large parts of several Book II chapters and most Book III chapters are. The most important essay in this context is perhaps "De la vanité" (III, ix).

To begin with, the title of the essay prepares us for a paradox. *Vanitas* means "nothing," and the "praise of nothing" was a favorite literary game in the Renaissance.[17] The "nothing," "emptiness" meaning underlies the use of *vanitas* in its celebrated biblical context but

---

[17] See Rosalie L. Colie, *Paradoxia Epidemica: The Renaissance Tradition of Paradox* (Princeton, N.J.: Princeton University Press, 1966), Part III; and Barbara Bowen, " 'Nothing' in French Renaissance Literature," *Kentucky Foreign Language Quarterly,* forthcoming.

is less obvious in the modern use of "vanity." So an essay about "nothing" which fills up pp. 945–1001 of the P.U.F. edition is likely to make the reader laugh before he has even started it. Many critics have analyzed the essay, finding different aspects to emphasize and differing over which of its three themes—vanity, traveling, the essays—is the essential one and which are the "disgressions."[18] In fact, the essay is one of the most unified Montaigne ever wrote and is based very simply on the analogy man's life/journey/essays. This is obvious in other essays from the frequency of the verb *aller* in expressions like "nous allons conformément et tout d'un trein, mon livre et moy" (III, ii, 806), and the second paragraph of "De la vanité" makes the analogy quite clear: "Qui ne voit que j'ay pris une *route* par laquelle, sans cesse et sans travail, *j'iray* autant qu'il y aura d'ancre et de papier au monde?" (p. 945; my italics). The road of the essays, like Montaigne's own travels, is not going anywhere in particular and could go on forever. But some idea of progress is inherent in the journey analogy; travel broadens the mind wherever the road is going, and a certain evolution is apparent in Montaigne's life as in his travels and his essays. My point is that the analogy book/man is essentially an artificial, literary one, to be taken not at face value but as a means of unifying the essays and of throwing light on both the man and the book.

It is quite clear from the context that this analogy is not to be taken seriously. Montaigne begins the essay on a mock-solemn note, quoting Scripture, but the first two sentences contradict each other. The second says that we should continually meditate on what Ecclesiastes has to say about vanity; the first says that the worst kind of vanity is to write about it. Granted that there is a difference between discussing vanity and discussing Scripture, what Montaigne is really doing here is playing on the two meanings of *vanitas,* the scriptural or positive meaning and the logical or scientific, negative meaning. The

---

18 See, for example, Pierre Moreau, *Montaigne, l'homme et l'oeuvre* (Paris: Boivin, 1939); Imbrie Buffum, *Studies in the Baroque from Montaigne to Rotrou* (New Haven, Conn.: Yale University Press, 1957); and Traeger, *Aufbau und Gedankenführung,* pp. 193–221.

first sentence is a fine tail-chaser of a paradox: vanity is itself empty, a "no-thing," so that writing about it must be emptier still, except that in so far as "nothing" provides a subject for writing, it ceases to be "nothing."

The third sentence is the one quoted above about his *route,* and the fourth states, "Je ne puis tenir registre de ma vie par mes actions: fortune les met trop bas," which is untrue. In the fifth sentence begins the analogy between the essays and "les excremens d'un vieil esprit," which surely the most ardent moralist could not take seriously. At the end of the paragraph, apropos of the grammarian Diomedes, he picks up the idea of the first sentence: "Tant de paroles pour les paroles seules!" This is a condemnation on moral grounds of grammarians and writers in general and of himself in particular, but it is also a fair enough statement of why he takes pleasure in writing.

The best way to discuss the essays is, of course, to examine them in detail, but let us first give some more thought to the general question, "What kind of artistic unit is an *essai?"* Now Montaigne's own pronouncements on this subject fall into two groups: the self-deprecating or my-style-is-clumsy-and-amateurish group, which has been well studied by recent critics, and the much less often noticed this-is-only-a-game group. Remarks belonging to the second group can also be self-deprecating but on the whole are not, although they are, or appear, lighthearted. Let us look carefully at some of these remarks, since they form an important body of evidence for a playful Montaigne.

In Book I there are already a number of remarks to this effect: an implication that he is as likely to use "le vraisemblable" as "le vrai" when telling a story (I, xxi, 105–6: *c*); an admiration for "vigueur" and "liberté," as opposed to subjection to rules and authority (I, xxvi, 151: *a* and *b*), and for the artistically symmetrical effects created by "le sort" (I, xxxiv, 221: *c*). A long passage at the beginning of I, l (301–2), sets out his method quite clearly: he likes to find something to say about a trivial subject or to see what remains to be said about a lofty and therefore much-discussed one; he takes "de la fortune le premier argument" and examines one aspect, preferably an unfamiliar one, of the subject under discussion—a clear statement, in fact, that his main preoccupation is the line of argument to be used. At the beginning of I, lvi (317: *a*), he tells us that his preoccupation is to seek truth, not to find it—a further emphasis on method as opposed to result or conclusion (cf. a similar remark at the beginning of II, iii, 350). Also in the course of I, lvi (323), he makes his celebrated distinction between "matière d'opinion" and "matière de foy," though in the context this remark is made from motives of prudence.

In II, x, he asserts firmly that he is not responsible for what he says (407: *a*) and in II, xii, as already mentioned, that he enjoys upholding contrary opinions, which sometimes change his mind for him (566: *b*). Later in this essay he reminds us that one can interpret a book in any number of different ways (585: *a*).

In Book III we find considerably more statements to the same effect, and in two essays he discusses criticisms which have been made of his first two books along these lines. In III, i (795: *b*), we learn that he has been accused of artistry rather than frankness, and in III, v, we find a very interesting list of condemnations of his work, including "Voilà un discours paradoxe" and "Tu te joues souvent" (875: *b* and *c*). This passage, if it can be taken at face value, is by itself a formidable argument in favor of my view of Montaigne. And a page later he tells us that he will say something one day for a joke and the next day in all seriousness, and that "Tout argument m'est egallement fertile."

The most important single essay from this point of view is III, viii. Modern critics seem to have forgotten Porteau's contention [19] that *conference* here means not conversation but debate or formal argument —"la pratique sportive de la contradiction." [20] Now what Montaigne says in this essay about the conduct of a debate is exactly what he says

[19] Paul Porteau, *Montaigne et la vie pédagogique de son temps* (Paris: Droz, 1935), ch. 18.

[20] *Ibid.*, p. 270. Further confirmation: in Abraham Fraunce's *The Arcadian Rhetorike* (1588), Book I, ch. 32, there is a discussion of "conference," or debating.

elsewhere about the *Essais*. He tells us that he enjoys being contradicted (p. 924); that the subject, opinions expressed, and result of the argument are indifferent to him (p. 925) because what matters is the dispute, not truth (pp. 927–28; anyone can tell the truth, but few people can organize a coherent argument); that he likes kidding (p. 938), that he doesn't even believe himself, and that "je hasarde souvent des boutades de mon esprit" (p. 943). These remarks are perfectly straightforward and unambiguous and amount to a firm double statement: that in an intellectual discussion it is the discussion itself that interests him, not its result, and that his general attitude to debate is essentially playful. The two halves of this declaration should be kept in mind because only the first half refers to aesthetics—the way in which an argument develops is or is not aesthetically pleasing, regardless of its content. The second half of the statement is an indication of an essentially humorous attitude of mind, and this is an aspect of Montaigne which has all too seldom been discussed.[21] Most of his readers are well aware that he is accustomed to see the funny side of things, to tell comic stories and make puns, and to emphasize the play aspect of things we normally regard as serious. Debate is one of these: most people become too involved in an argument, thereby losing their effectiveness as debaters. The discussion will be both more fun and more effective, says Montaigne, if we don't take it too seriously.

These remarks on verbal debate, then, are entirely similar to the previously quoted statements about the *Essais,* and there are more such statements in Book III. In III, ix, he tells us how much he prefers spontaneity, real or apparent, to things learned by heart and that he doesn't like a classically organized oration (963); in III, xi, he says that though he doesn't lie, he does often exaggerate and amplify (1028) and that he treats everything "par maniere de devis" (1033); and in III, xiii, he says, "J'ay un dictionaire tout à part moy" (1111).

21 See K. C. Cameron, *Montaigne et l'humour,* Archives des Lettres Modernes, no. 71 (Paris: Minard, 1966), a short and superficial study; and Donald Nolan's unpublished dissertation, "Montaigne's Use of the Comic in the *Essais*" (University of Illinois, Urbana, 1967).

All these statements add up to a very solid body of evidence that Montaigne's tongue is firmly is his cheek while writing. With this in mind, let us look again at some of his deprecating descriptions of the essays. I do not need to demonstrate the falseness of his remarks about his style, which has been abundantly discussed by recent critics.[22] But if he is joking about his style, why should we assume that apparently pejorative references to the essays as "fagotage" (II, xxxvii, 758), "fricassée" (III, xiii, 1079), and "une marqueterie mal jointe" (III, ix, 964) are to be taken seriously? *Fagotage* is the art of tying up pieces of wood ("trussing up in bundles"—Cotgrave), which, as anyone who has tried knows, is not as easy as it looks. A *fricassée* is a stew, and what Frenchman would deny skill and artistry to a cook? And, as I have explained elsewhere, *marqueterie* is most unlikely to be an inlaid floor, the artistry of which is apparent from any angle.[23] It is probably a synonym for "mosaic," which looks like a jumble of little stones when you are close to it but, when you step back, reveals a beautiful design or picture. So at this point a further puzzling element is introduced. Is Montaigne deprecating his essays by the use of such terms, or is he slyly indicating that he, in fact, uses a great deal of artistry, although the casual reader might not think so?

Let us look a little more closely at the "marqueterie mal jointe" passage (p. 964). Here it is in context:

b) Laisse, lecteur, courir encore ce coup d'essay et ce troisiesme allongeail du reste des pieces de ma peinture. J'adjouste, mais je ne corrige pas. Premierement, par ce que celuy qui a hypothecqué au monde son ouvrage, je trouve apparence qu'il n'y aye plus de droict. Qu'il die, s'il peut, mieux ailleurs, et ne corrompe la besongne qu'il a venduë. De telles gens il ne faudroit rien acheter

---

[22] In particular Gray and Buffum; Michael Baraz, "Les images dans les *Essais* de Montaigne," *BHR* XXVII (1965), 361–94 (reproduced in Part I, ch. 3, of his book); Jean Starobinski, "Montaigne en mouvement," *NRF* (Jan.–Mar. 1960), pp. 16–22, 254–66; and Sayce, "Montaigne et la peinture du passage."

[23] Barbara Bowen, "What Does Montaigne Mean by *marqueterie?*" *SP* LXVII (1970), 147–55.

qu'apres leur mort. Qu'ils y pensent bien avant que de se produire. Qui les haste?

c) Mon livre est tousjours un. Sauf qu'à mesure qu'on se met à le renouveller, afin que l'acheteur ne s'en aille les mains du tout vuides, je me donne loy d'y attacher (comme ce n'est qu'une marqueterie mal jointe), quelque embleme supernumeraire. Ce ne sont que surpoids, qui ne condamnent point la premiere forme, mais donnent quelque pris particulier à chacune des suivantes par une petite subtilité ambitieuse. De là toutesfois il adviendra facilement qu'il s'y mesle quelque transposition de chronologie, mes contes prenans place selon leur opportunité, non tousjours selon leur aage.

The first paragraph already has a slightly tongue-in-cheek tone. There are many elements worth commenting upon in the first sentence, the most playful of them being the contradiction between *courir* and *peinture* and the emphasis on *pieces*—his portrait is not a whole but an assemblage of elements (like a mosaic or inlaid floor composed of *pièces rapportées*). *J'adjouste, mais je ne corrige pas* is not strictly true, even before 1588, and is in any case a false antithesis. Many of his additions are also corrections. We shall meet many examples of this later on, particularly in "Des menteurs" where the *b* version gives a completely different dimension to the essay.

The following sentence contains an apparently valid reason for not correcting, but Montaigne does not abide by it—if he had, he would have written three separate essays on each subject discussed in Book I, instead of adding later reflections to the first version. And the rest of this paragraph is a similar self-condemnation.

The added paragraph begins with a remark in direct contradiction to his statements about his book's evolution and diversity. He then makes an excuse for the additions he now has to admit to. Now the main problem of the *marqueterie* analogy is this: is Montaigne thinking primarily of the visual effect produced by a mosaic floor or of the technique of its construction? In the first case *embleme* must mean an element of the design, whereas in the second case it would have to be a piece of stone (or less probably wood) used by the craftsman.[24] In any case, the expression "marqueterie mal jointe" is particularly interesting. It puts the emphasis on the construction of the essays and the joining together of their different parts. Montaigne does this elsewhere by drawing attention to his digressions, additions, and changes of subject. Remarks like "Je dy donc, pour revenir à mon propos" (II, xii, 460), "Mais je m'en vois un peu bien à gauche de mon theme" (II, xxvii, 699), "Revenons à noz bouteilles" (II, ii, 344), and "Retombons à nos coches" (III, vi, 915) are frequent and are intended to emphasize the jumbled, spontaneous aspect of the *Essais*. But a *marqueterie*, like a *fagotage* and a *fricassée*, is a work of art, so we have here the same kind of ambivalence we have noted elsewhere. In the rest of this paragraph, moreover, Montaigne appears to be excusing the procedure he apparently condemns in the parenthesis.

I would suggest, then, that the pejorative connotation normally assigned to these words is unjustified, and that Montaigne is, in fact, emphasizing the artistry of the essays while appearing to condemn them for lack of artistry. This conclusion is borne out by some remarks of Montaigne's about Plato.

It is generally assumed that Montaigne's admiration for Plato does not extend to the form of the dialogues, described in II, x (414), as "trainans" and "ces longues interlocutions vaines et preparatoires." This would certainly appear to be a condemnation of some of the dialogues—they vary greatly in length and tone. But another remark of Montaigne's which has been similarly interpreted may not be a condemnation: he refers in III, ix, to the *Phaedrus* as "mi party d'une fantastique bigarrure, le devant à l'amour, tout le bas à la rhetorique" (994). Why should *bigarrure* be pejorative here? In the *Journal de voyage* Montaigne gives the following description of the tessellated roofs of Bâle: "Ils sont aussi excellens en tuilleries, de façon que les

---

24 This seems more likely, according to Huguet and Littré.

couvertures des maisons sont fort embellies de bigarrures de tuillerie plombée en divers ouvrages," which is clearly not pejorative.[25] The analogy of the *Phaedrus* to a tessellated roof is very similar to the analogy between the *Essais* and a mosaic floor, and the connection between Montaigne and Plato is worth examining.

Montaigne's admiration for Socrates the man has often been noted and is certainly an important element of the *Essais*.[26] What has been less emphasized is his admiration for Socrates the debater, which fits in perfectly with the tongue-in-cheek statements about the essays which we have been discussing. The non-Classicist reading Plato's dialogues is struck most forcibly by the playful aspect of the whole technique: Socrates frequently refuses to conclude an argument because he doesn't really believe his own reasoning (*Charmide*); often twists the meaning of a quotation to suit the purpose of his argument (*Protagoras,* xxxi); often uses analogy which is difficult to justify logically; and is constantly accused of irony and mockery by his interlocutors. The content of the dialogues is usually serious enough, but their form and tone are often humorous, and Montaigne makes it clear that he appreciated this. In III, v, he tells us that "Socrates eut un visage constant, mais serein et riant" (845); in III, viii, we see him "tousjours riant" (925); and in III, xii, the most important essay for Socrates, Montaigne says that when he talked of the ugliness of his soul, "je tiens qu'il se mocquoit suivant son usage" (1058). This last quotation, a *c* addition, suggests the technique as being humorous as well as the man —Socrates was readily admitted to have been a joker (cf. Rabelais's prologue to *Gargantua*). Montaigne is not thereby devaluating Socrates' moral teaching. On the contrary, as Horace said, "Ridentem dicere verum Quid vetat?" (III, v, 877), and stupidity and seriousness go together: "Est il rien certein, resolu, desdeigneux, contemplatif, grave, serieux come l'asne?" (III, viii, 938).

[25] Reprinted in Montaigne, *Oeuvres complètes,* ed. A. Thibaudet and M. Rat (Paris: Bibliothèque de la Pléiade, 1962), p. 1130.

[26] See above, note 14, and Baraz's article "Sur la structure d'un essai de Montaigne (III, 13)," *BHR* XXIII (1961), 265–81 (reproduced in his book).

In view of the similarity between the aspects of Plato's technique mentioned above and the aspects of the *Essais* which we have been discussing, it seems reasonable to suppose that Montaigne has Plato in mind when talking about his own technique. In any case, all the words we have mentioned—*fagotage, fricassée, marqueterie,* and *bigar-rure*—are ambiguous and provide support for the theory that Montaigne is bluffing his reader into underestimating the structure of the *Essais*.[27] The same applies to the painter's "crotesques" surrounding the central motif of a picture (I, xxviii, 183), which clearly must be artistically ordered or they would not be effective. Butor has taken the *crotesques* seriously and discusses them at length, but does not mention their affinity to all the other words which are similarly ambivalent.[28]

We must also remember the frequency of words like *bastir, coudre,* and *contexture* in the *Essais*—an emphasis on construction and co-herence and a complete contradiction to the apparent denial of structure in expressions like "marqueterie mal jointe." We should not forget *peindre* either, in this connection; a self-portrait, if it has any artistic merit, is necessarily "composed," and I have tried to show that this is true of Montaigne's.

The conclusion to all this seems so obvious that I hesitate to under-line it: Montaigne's whole attitude to himself, his book, and his reader is tongue in cheek. His moral attitude is often serious but is disguised by its form, his intellectual attitude is analytical and often playful, and his artistic attitude delights in paradox and ambiguity. His acknowledg-ments to Plato, his own remarks about the *Essais* and the kind of *conference* he prefers, are all ambivalent, and the tone of all of them indicates a love of ambiguity for its own sake. This, of course, coexists with frequent moralizing denunciations of ambiguity in our thought processes, which is the aspect of ambiguity normally emphasized by critics. What I am suggesting is that it is less important for Montaigne

---

[27] See S. J. Holyoake, "Further Reflections on Montaigne and the Concept of the Imagination," *BHR* XXXI (1969), 515, note 57.
[28] Butor, *Essais sur les Essais*, p. 66.

as a writer than the playful delight in ambivalence, and I think a more
detailed study of individual essays will provide support for this contention.

Turning finally to the essays as individual works of art, let us begin
with Book I. And here I would like to demolish another ancient myth,
the myth of the great gulf fixed between the earlier essays and the
later ones. With only one exception that I know of,[29] every single
critic of Montaigne refers disparagingly to the first essays as "compilations," as "centons de lectures" in which nothing is personal or
original.[30] Examination of the essays shows that this is a gross exag-
geration; in any case, the pejorative tone of these remarks seems to
me irrelevant. What does it matter what examples Montaigne uses and
where they come from? Is it really more original to talk about one's
own fussy eating habits than about the military strategy of Caesar and
Pompey? What does matter is how the examples are used and what
Montaigne is really talking about. Certainly in the early essays he
quotes a great deal, but his literary examples serve the same purpose
there as do his personal examples in the later essays. Certainly there
are long lists and itemizations of oddities, events, or opinions, but in
nearly every case these lists contain paradoxes, contradictions, and
different levels of thought. The only essays which could be described
as straightforward compilations are I, xxxvi ("De l'usage de se vestir"),
I, xlviii ("Des destries"), I, xlix ("Des coustumes anciennes"), I, lv
("Des senteurs"), II, xxii ("Des postes"), and II, xxvi ("Des pouces").
Other essays which might on a superficial reading give the impression
of compilations are, in fact, much more than that, like I, xi ("Des prognostications"), which in the first edition is very short. However, the *a*

---

[29] Traeger, *Aufbau und Gedankenführung.*

[30] See, most recently, Baraz, *L'être et la connaissance,* p. 54: "La plupart de ces
chapitres sont des centons d'exemples livresques."

text already contains a paradox (oracles are dead, but look how superstitious the Marquis de Sallusse was), and the essay forms part of an important group (I, v–vii and ix–xi) whose subject is *la parole*. Book I, essays v and vi, discuss the literal usage of *la parole* ("word of honor") and its place in war; I, vii, discusses whether death releases one from the obligation imposed by this word of honor; I, ix, examines the whole question of lying; I, x, compares and contrasts "le parler prompt" and "le parler tardif"; and I, xi, considers oracles because they are an example of authoritative but mysterious *parole*, and they raise the question of whether we should accept or reject this particular form of suprahuman speech.

A close look at the first essay, "Par divers moyens on arrive à pareille fin," will show that as early as 1577–78 (Villey's date) Montaigne uses much the same method he will always use.[31] This is certainly not the first essay he wrote, but it is the one he chose to introduce his book to the reader. The title contains his favorite word, *divers,* and a paradox: you would expect *different* means to produce *different* results, but this is not always the case. In the *a* text the argument goes like this: The most usual way to soften the hearts of vengeful enemies is to incite them to pity by one's humility. *But* the *contrary* attitude of courage can have the same effect. For instance, Edward, Prince of Wales, was moved to pity not by cries for mercy but by courageous resistance. Similarly, Scanderberch pardoned a soldier who defended himself. However, Scanderberch's motive just might have been cowardice rather than respect for courage ("Cet exemple pourra souffrir autre interpretation . . . ," p. 8). The Emperor Conrad was also moved to pity by the magnanimity of the women who carried their men out of the city. These examples suggest that the pity of these men, induced by esteem, is nobler than the pity "des femmes, des enfans et du vulgaire," which is really weakness. *However,* in less noble souls amazement can produce the same effect as esteem in noble ones. For instance, the Thebans

---

[31] After writing my analysis of this essay, I discovered that Friedrich had long ago written a similar, though less detailed, one (*Montaigne,* pp. 158–60).

condemned Pelopidas, who implored mercy, and absolved Epaminondas, who refused even to defend himself. Man is indeed "un subject
merveilleusement vain, divers et ondoyant" (p. 9). Pompey and Sylla
reacted quite differently to similar admonitions to clemency made in
similar circumstances.[32]

This argument is by no means banal, nor is it a straightforward
opposition between two possible attitudes. The noble-respect-for-virtue
attitude is qualified by the doubt over Scanderberch's motive; a further complication is introduced with the addition of *estonnement* as a
motive in the case of the Thebans; and the conclusion on the vanity
and diversity of man will be a major theme of the *Essais*. It is also
typical of the *Essais* that even in the *a* text the conclusion is followed
by an extra example of the argument.

The main outline of the essay looks like this:

GENERAL REFLECTION > three opposing examples with one qualifi-
cation > GENERAL REFLECTION ("Or, ces exemples . . .") > CON-
TRADICTORY REFLECTION ("Toutesfois ès ames moins genereuses")
> two opposing examples > CONCLUSION > two opposing ex-
amples.

The length and number of the examples are not symmetrical, but the
structure is balanced by the alternation of statement and example, and
the development of the argument is perfectly clear.

The first *b* addition, inserted between the Emperor Conrad and
the Thebans, contains a personal reference and adds two paradoxes:
I could be moved to pity in either case because I am a gentle person by
nature. Compassion would probably be a stronger motive than esteem
in my case; *however,* the Stoics condemn pity as a "passion vitieuse."

[32] The source, Plutarch's *Instruction pour ceulx qui manient affaires d'état*, LXI (and
not XVII as the Villey edition states), is clearer than Montaigne's version. Pompey's
host, Stheno, persuaded him not to punish a whole city for the fault of a few; Sylla
condemned the whole city of Praeneste except his host, who refused this immunity and
perished with the others. The two situations are not symmetrically opposed in Plutarch
as they are in Montaigne.

This addition breaks the thread of the argument and introduces an element tending to contradict the whole essay, which tacitly assumed, in the *a* text, that pity is evidence of virtue. If the Stoics are right in condemning pity, however, then even the men approved in the *a* version are not admirable.

The second *b* addition is much longer (p. 9), follows what was the end of the essay in *a*, and specifically introduces a further contradiction: "Et directement *contre* mes premiers exemples." The contradictory example is that of Alexander, who was moved not to compassion but to further cruelty by the courage of his victim. And the essay now ends on a question: was this because courage was such an ordinary thing for him that he didn't respect it?

The first *c* addition is a short insertion in the description of Epaminondas's refusal to justify himself to the Thebans (p. 8). By adding "d'une façon fiere et arrogante" Montaigne underlines the suggestion, already present in the *a* text, that Epaminondas's conduct was not, in fact, very praiseworthy. Elsewhere (in particular in "Des plus excellens hommes" and "De l'utile et de l'honneste") Epaminondas is treated as a hero, but there is a pejorative note here in *magnifiquement, fiere,* and *arrogante.*

The next *c* insertion is a long paragraph on Dionysius which comes after the sentence on Epaminondas and before the original conclusion. Dionysius, in circumstances similar to Alexander's in the *b* insert, realized that Phyton's courage was being approved and his own cruelty condemned, stopped torturing him, and had him drowned secretly. This is not a contradiction so much as another aspect of the cruelty/clemency question. Dionysius is moved neither by compassion nor admiration but by expediency: the torture of Phyton is not having the expected effect on the soldiers.

The final *c* addition follows the end of the essay in *b,* which was a question. To the suggested motive for Alexander's lack of compassion, that he didn't respect courage, Montaigne now adds two other

possible motives: either he was jealous of Betis's courage or he was
angered by it and regarded it as an obstacle that must be overcome.
And the essay ends, in the form in which we have it, with a description of the courage of the defeated defenders of Thebes, to show that
if Alexander was not moved to pity at that time, he must have been
incapable of pity.

In its final form the essay is considerably longer and more difficult
to follow than it was to start with, and its overall pattern now looks
like this:

> GENERAL REFLECTION > three opposing examples with one qualifi-
> cation > personal example with paradox which is another GENERAL
> REFLECTION > GENERAL REFLECTION ("Or, ces exemples . . .") >
> CONTRADICTORY REFLECTION > two opposing examples > contra-
> dictory example (Dionysius) > CONCLUSION > two opposing
> examples > example (Alexander) contradicting earlier ones >
> discussion of Alexander's conduct.

The relative symmetry of the *a* text has been destroyed; the conclusion,
which began by being very near the end of the essay, is now close to its
center, and further paradoxical elements have been introduced to dis-
tract from the original cruelty/clemency issue. But in spite of all this
the subject of discussion has not changed, the conclusion remains what
it always was, and the illustrations of the vanity and diversity of man
are all variations on the cruelty/clemency issue. Paradoxes have been
added, but the *a* text already contained several, and Montaigne's attitude to the problem has not changed between 1577 and 1595: his main
purpose in all three versions is to show us that the cruelty/clemency
antithesis is an oversimplification and hence false, since neither cruelty
nor clemency is always what it seems. The essay is as much a discussion of human nature as is an essay from Book III; the difference is
in tone, not in subject matter or in basic preoccupations. The Montaigne nosing around the different aspects of cruelty versus clemency

in 1577 is the same Montaigne who will be turning over the problem of experience in 1588.

In nearly all the essays of Book I the *a* text contains basic paradoxes or contradictions, which will certainly be added to or developed in *b* and *c*. But it is simply not true that the *a* text is uninteresting and gives no indication of what Montaigne will later become. The *a* text of I, iii ("Nos affections s'emportent au dela de nous"), is very short but contains several examples of paradox and a charming *boutade* as conclusion ("Il devoit adjouster par codicille, que celuy qui les [des calessons quand il seroit mort] luy monteroit eut les yeux bandez," p. 19). "Qu'il ne faut juger de nostre heur, qu'après la mort" (I, xix) has as its title Solon's remark to Croesus, which is itself a paradox, and in the *a* text Montaigne adds to it a reinterpretation of this remark in the light of Stoicism (p. 79): the only possible judgment on a man's life is the way in which he dies because that is the only situation in which he must be sincere: "En tout le reste il y peut avoir du masque." The *b* and *c* additions mainly concern the Stoic attitude to death, which is not altogether compatible with the original paradox, but my point is that the *a* text is already concerned with paradox.

An interesting case is that of "Des menteurs" (I, ix), which the *b* and *c* additions apparently transform into something completely different from the original version. Both Villey and Frame would put this among the earliest essays Montaigne wrote, so according to traditional theory, the *a* text would not be very interesting. It is certainly a good deal less interesting than the final version, but it contains exactly the tongue-in-cheek tone which will pervade the final essay. The title leads us to expect a neatly organized condemnation of lying in the rhetorical tradition, but here is Montaigne's first paragraph:

> Il n'est homme a qui il siese si mal de se mesler de parler de la memoire qu'a moy. Car je n'en reconnoy quasi nulle trasse chez moy, et ne pense qu'il y en aye au monde une si monstrueuse en defaillance. J'ai toutes mes autres parties villes et communes; mais

en cete la je pense estre singulier et tresrare, et digne de gaigner par
la nom et reputation. J'en pourrois faire des contes merveilleus,
mais, pour cete heure, il vaut mieux suivre mon theme.[33]

In the first place it is not immediately obvious why an essay on liars
should begin by talking about memory. A moment's reflection will
suggest the connection—memory is one of the five divisions of Ciceronian rhetoric, and rhetoric has obvious connections with lying—but the
reader's first reaction is one of surprise. Second, one does not expect a
personal note at the beginning of a discussion on a banal moral *topos,*
and third, this personal note is exaggeratedly self-deprecating. The
word *monstrueuse* is comically out of proportion to a minor defect like
lack of memory, but, together with the succession of negatives in the
first two sentences, it prepares us for the fourth. The third sentence
picks up the pejorative note of the first two (*siese si mal, monstrueuse
en defaillance*) and exaggerates it still further: *J'ai toutes mes autres
parties villes et communes.* This sentence looks like the minor premise
of a pseudosyllogism which would run like this: "My memory is ter-
rible. My other faculties are not much good either. Therefore I am
altogether worthless." But in the next sentence Montaigne reverses
his own argument (*Mais . . .*), so that the conclusion is not "I am
altogether worthless" but "My memory is so uniquely bad that it
makes me worthy of respect rather than condemnation." *Singulier,
rare, nom,* and *reputation* are all neutral words and hence ambiguous,
since they can apply to qualities either remarkably good or remarkably bad. And we perceive that the opposition here is not, as we had
thought, between good qualities and bad qualities but between ordinary qualities (*villes et communes*) shared by everybody and extraordinary qualities unique to Montaigne. In the light of this fourth
sentence the *villes et communes* of the third loses its ethically pejorative connotation and acquires in retrospect the more neutral meaning of "belonging to the common herd." Similarly, the *monstrueuse*

---

[33] This is the text given in the Dezeimeris and Barckhausen edition (Paris, 1870–
73), p. 20.

of sentence 2 loses most of its pejorative force, since anything mon-strous is unique, and the unique words of the fourth sentence are apparently not pejorative. I say "apparently" because there is genuine ambiguity here; is Montaigne condemning his uniquely bad memory, or is he praising it because it marks him off from the common herd? The second interpretation seems more likely in view of the progression from clearly pejorative (*defaillance*) to barely pejorative (*tresrare*) words, and in view of the *merveilleus* of the next sentence. However, Montaigne deleted this sentence in 1588, perhaps to increase the am-biguity of the first paragraph. It seems rather a pity that he did delete it because *il vaut mieux suivre mon theme* is charming—the reader has no idea at this point what his theme is.

The *a* text goes on (p. 35 in the Villey-Saulnier edition) to clarify the connection between memory and lying, the one being clearly necessary to the other. There follows a distinction, which Montaigne apparently does not think much of, between involuntary lying (*men-songe*) and voluntary lying (*mentir*), which is what Montaigne is talking about. He then divides liars into two groups (p. 36), those who invent everything and those who distort a foundation of truth. The latter operation is tricky because the original truth is stronger than the superstructure of lies which have to be kept in the memory. The former operation is easier but still depends on memory because a com-plete fabrication of lies is "un corps vain et sans prise." And the last two paragraphs of the *a* text give, at length (pp. 37–38), illustrations of how hazardous lying is.

Nowhere in the *a* text is there any discussion of the moral impli-cations of lying. Montaigne begins with ambiguous statements about his lack of memory, goes on to an analysis of different types of lying, and ends with examples of the difficulty of lying successfully. We are clearly meant to conclude that Montaigne is a truthful person because his memory is so bad, and we are clearly intended to make the con-nection between this essay and the other essays on speech in its group— memory is a division of rhetoric, and Sforza's *science de parlerie* is mentioned on p. 37. Short as it is, the essay already contains paradoxes, ambiguities, shifts of viewpoint, and an analytical approach. To those who would say that lying is a simple activity straightforwardly opposed to telling the truth, Montaigne replies that lying is not simple, can be divided into different categories, and requires memory and a quick wit. The implication is clear that it takes a smart man to be a good liar, and Montaigne could well be saying at the beginning of the essay that the only reason he doesn't lie is that he has too poor a memory.[34] Another implication already present in the *a* version is that lying is a positive as well as a negative activity. In Burke's words a lie is "creative" in the sense that it adds to reality.[35] An educated Renaissance reader would certainly be familiar with the paradox of the liar attributed to Epimenides—if a man says "I am a liar," is he or isn't he? The absence of negative moral strictures on lying suggests that Montaigne is more interested in these positive aspects.

The final state of the essay is proof that the subject continued to fascinate him. The first *b* addition discusses the assertion that lack of memory equals lack of common sense. On the contrary, says Montaigne as usual, "il se voit par experience . . . que les memoires excellentes se joignent volontiers aux jugemens debiles," one of the major themes of "De l'institution des enfants." He then gives an example of the disadvantages of a bad memory: one can lose friends through simple forgetfulness. So this paragraph contains a plea *for* bad memory (since it often goes with superior intelligence) and a plea *against* it. He then goes on to the consolations of bad memory, the first being that he cannot speak at great length and bore his listeners (p. 35). The antithesis between *memoire* and *jugement* is reiterated here. The second consolation is that he doesn't bear grudges because he doesn't remember the offense, and the third that he is not bored by places and books he has already seen because they always seem new to him.

[34] Brewer's *Dictionary of Phrase and Fable*, 8th ed. (1963), art. *Liar*, gives "Liars should have good memories" as an old proverb, found in Quintilian and St. Jerome.
[35] Kenneth Burke, *A Grammar of Motives* (Berkeley and Los Angeles: University of California Press, 1969), p. 174.

The remaining *b* addition is a development of the *a* paragraph on different kinds of liars (p. 36) and a further explanation of why lying as a profession ("cette belle art") is so hazardous. People who try to adapt their speech (*parole* again) to the "grands à qui ils parlent" may think they are being prudent, but their memories cannot be good enough to enable them to get away with it. There is an implication here that *les grands* do have good memories and hence may well be scoundrels.

The *b* additions, then, concentrate on the positive aspects of lack of memory and on the futility of lying. The tone is even less moralizing here than in the first version, but the *c* text will more than restore the balance. The first *c* addition is just a passing Classical allusion, but the second (p. 34) adds a consolation at the head of the *b* list: lack of memory is an evil, but it's a safeguard against a worse evil, ambition. Memory is indispensable for "qui s'empesche des negotiations du monde," and he might have been tempted in this direction if he had been capable of it. The next *c* passage, illustrating the first *b* consolation (that people with no memory can't talk at any length), describes how he would have "assourdi tous mes amys de babil" if his memory had permitted. Incidentally, the "C'est pitié" of the next *b* sentence, which originally applied to the fact that memory is a "magasin . . . plus fourny de matiere" than invention, now appears to apply to Montaigne's habit of embroidering upon subjects of conversation.

The following *c* addition develops this subject further and compares the intemperate talker to a horse which can't stop when it should. The next is an illustration on the subject of remembering grievances, but the last is a long and frankly moral conclusion to the essay, although it is inserted before the *a* illustration of people who tie themselves in knots over their lies. Montaigne finally makes the ethical judgment we have been expecting all along: "En vérité le mentir est un maudit vice," and explains how lying fits into this group of essays on speech: "Nous ne sommes hommes et ne nous tenons les uns aux autres que par la parole." So lying, as well as foolish, ill advised, and difficult, is also wrong in the most fundamental sense—it is a *perversion* of speech, which is what distinguishes man from beast. We should be very careful, says Montaigne, to punish lying rigorously, especially in children, because it is a habit which, once acquired, is very difficult to get rid of. He adds two paradoxes, the "honnestes hommes d'ailleurs" who are slaves to the habit of lying, and the "bon garçon de tailleur" who cannot tell the truth even when it would be in his interest to do so. Finally, he adds two subsidiary conclusions in passing: the basic problem is that truth is one but falsehood diverse, so we cannot just believe the opposite of what the liar says, and silence is more sociable than unknown or counterfeit language.

I said above that the essay is *apparently* very different as we now have it from its first version, but is this really the case? The *b* additions certainly weight the argument in favor of lack of memory, but the implication that lack of memory is not necessarily a disadvantage was already present in *a*. And the explicit moral conclusions of *c* were also present in the tone of *a*. It is typical of Montaigne that not until the third version of the essay does he draw the moral conclusion we expected when we saw the title, and that when he does give it, his reason is unexpected: lying is a *maudit vice,* not because the Church says so but because it is a negation of man's essential nature and value.

I have analyzed this essay at such length because I think it demolishes two of the most deeply rooted myths about Montaigne. It shows that there is not a gulf fixed between *a* and *c,* that the tone remains the same through three versions, though the emphasis may shift, and that the *a* text contains by implication everything that is in the final version. As well as adding to this essay in *c,* Montaigne wrote another on the same subject, "De l'utile et de l'honneste" (III, i), which is very similar in tone, though it explores more aspects of the subject. Second, this essay shows that from the very beginning

Montaigne's propensity for paradox and ambiguity was likely to disconcert the reader.

There is one more important idea to be stated about "Des menteurs." Going back for a moment to the first sentence, "Il n'est homme a qui il siese si mal de se mesler de parler de memoire qu'a moy," we see that, admitting that talking about memory is the same thing as talking about lying, which it certainly seems to be for Montaigne, this first sentence in a sense cancels out the entire essay. Montaigne begins, in fact, by disqualifying himself for talking about the subject of the essay. This might be involuntary but is more probably a deliberate *boutade,* particularly as there are several other examples of it in each book of the *Essais.* Chapter liv of Book I, "Des vaines subtilitez," begins with a firm condemnation of them, while the rest of the essay complacently enumerates examples of them. And chapter xxx, "De la moderation," is a curious case. The first two-thirds of it (pp. 197–200) read like a plea for moderation, and the last third (from "Mais, à parler en bon escient" on p. 200) like a condemnation of it ("La sagesse humaine faict bien sottement l'ingenieuse de s'exercer à rabattre le nombre et la douceur des voluptez qui nous appartiennent"). These are the most striking examples in Book I of essays which cancel themselves out; the most striking example of all is, of course, the "Apologie de Raymond Sebond," which sets out to defend an author who had upheld the validity of human reason in matters of faith and ends by demolishing the validity of human reason in any domain whatever.

The two essays I have discussed in detail (I, i and ix) show clearly that from the beginning one of Montaigne's main concerns was to disconcert and puzzle his reader. A close study of the other essays in Book I would show that in almost every case a paradox is present, either in the title or in the *a* text; that a large number of them deal with the contradiction between what he will call "le nom et la chose" (II, xvi, 618); that "Des noms" (I, xlvi) is a discussion of the conventional nature of language; and that many of them contain puns, jokes, and *boutades*. I have spent a good deal of time on Book I because the essays in it have to my mind been consistently underestimated. They often contain as much complexity and food for thought as the later essays, but they lack the detailed development which will make the essays of Book III easier to read. Some of them look rather like "notes for a discussion on . . . ," and the modern reader, who knows from Book III how Montaigne's mind is likely to work, has an advantage over the reader of 1580, who must sometimes have been puzzled.

BOOK II

All of the above is equally true of the shorter essays of Book II. The longer ones have been far more discussed, particularly, of course, the "Apologie," which is fascinating but not at all typical of Montaigne's thought or structure. Many of the shorter ones deserve equally exhaustive treatment, but I should like to stress II, i, "Des livres" (II, x), and "Du dementir" (II, xviii).

II, i, begins the book with *inconstance*, as I, i, began with *diversité*. II, i, is also an early essay (about 1572, according to Villey), but it has a very different structure from that of I, ix, for instance. It appears at first sight to consist of a series of illustrations of the title, but a closer examination shows that it is more complex than this and that it has a unity based on several different analogies. The first of these analogies is between individual human actions and "pieces" (at the end of the first paragraph on p. 332), and the words *piece* and *lopin* (p. 337) recur throughout the essay, suggesting that for Montaigne the human personality is simply a jumble of heterogeneous elements with no unifying principle. However, the verb *r'appiesser* (p. 331) means "to fit pieces together," and *pieces rapportees* (p. 336) has a technical meaning in carpentry.[36] We then notice that another key word in this essay, as in many others, is *contexture* (pp. 332, 337), which Larousse explains as "liaison des parties d'un tout." So it seems that for Montaigne our actions appear inconstant, not because they have no underlying unity but because we do not perceive this unity, a different matter altogether. In the much-quoted *a* sentence "Nous sommes tous de lopins, et d'une contexture si informe et diverse . . ." (p. 337) the emphasis is normally placed on *lopins*. But the point is that the *lopins* are part of the *contexture* and that there *is* a *contexture*, however *informe et diverse* it may be. So what looks to us like an individual action or trait bearing no relation to a whole is, in fact, part of a design whose outline we cannot see. For practical purposes this comes to the same thing: we still cannot imagine why so-and-so did such-and-such, but Montaigne seems to be putting the emphasis on an appearance of inconstancy rather than a real inconstancy.

So the essay already has a kind of tension between *piece* and *contexture*. It also has an apparent contradiction between the static *piece-contexture-masque* images and the metaphors of moving and traveling.[37] In the *a* text the first paragraph contains *r'appiesser* and *assortir ces pieces*, and the next two paragraphs contain *voie, aller, le vent . . . nous emporte, retournons sur nos pas, allons, emporte, flottent, se meuvent*, and *mouvemens*. There is a tension here too, as Starobinski points out, between purposeful movement (*allons, retournons sur nos pas*) and involuntary or passive movement (*on nous emporte*), often associated with wind ("le vent des occasions nous emporte") or water ("les choses qui flottent . . . selon que l'eau est ireuse ou bonasse"). There are many other metaphors in the essay, but these are the dominant ones, and they are used in all three stages of the text. The *b* and

[36] See above, p. 124, and my article cited in note 22.
[37] See Starobinski, "Montaigne en mouvement." Philip Hallie also talks about "a tension between change and stability, between diversity and unity, between spontaneity and control" (*The Scar of Montaigne*, p. 101), and Friedrich, Baraz, and Holyoake make similar remarks. What I am maintaining is that Montaigne is *playing* with these tensions.

c additions do not change the emphasis of the essay; they give more information on Montaigne's "contrarietez" (p. 335) and add examples and discussion. The essay is in fact very unified when compared with "Des menteurs" and is held together in all three stages by the interplay of metaphor. This confirms what I said above about *contexture*— the essay is an example of a *contexture* which appears *informe et diverse* but is in fact not so.

One might also consider this very unity of the essay as a *boutade* —the essay is called "De l'inconstance de nos actions," but it underlines the constancy of this inconstancy, so to speak—and it ends with a *boutade* which has the effect, already discussed, of canceling out the entire essay. The last sentence, which is *a,* says that since unworthy motives can produce acts of heroism and virtue, "ce n'est pas tour de rassis entendement de nous juger simplement par nos actions de dehors; il faut sonder jusqu'au dedans, et voir par quels ressors se donne le bransle; mais, d'autant que c'est une hazardeuse et haute entreprinse, je voudrois que moins de gens s'en meslassent." What has Montaigne been doing throughout the essay, if not *s'en mesler?* So to the tension and contradiction inherent in his metaphors he adds, in the final words of the essay, an admonition apparently directed at himself and certainly intended to make the reader laugh and think twice.

"Des livres" (II, x) is a later essay (about 1579, according to Villey) chiefly concerned with Montaigne's own preference in books. But the first few pages (407–10) contain some deprecating remarks about his book, typical of this period, and what looks like one of the boldest *boutades* he ever made.

He begins with an apology for his essays, which are *fantasies,* not *science,* and "fantasies, par lesquelles je ne tasche point à donner à connoistre les choses, mais moy." This kind of remark has always been taken quite seriously by Montaigne's commentators; it looks to me like an *échappatoire*—if he says his main purpose is self-portraiture, he will not risk criticisms on other grounds. Similarly, in the *c* addi-

tion on p. 408 he escapes the accusation of plagiarism by freely admitting it. Moreover, he manages, as so often, to turn the argument
around; on p. 407 he apologizes for his ignorance but on 409 (also *a*)
points out that "la reconnoissance de l'ignorance est l'un des plus
beaux et plus seurs tesmoignages de jugement que je trouve." So what
looked like a self-accusation has turned into self-praise.

The next few paragraphs are an apology for his casual and superficial manner of reading, and the passage on Aesop on p. 410 suggests
that it is better to read superficially than to find deep hidden meanings which the author did not intend. So once again the apparent apology will turn out to be a justification. The penultimate paragraph on
p. 409 contains a very entertaining analogy between reading and an
activity which is not normally compared to it. Montaigne had first
written in the *a* text, "Les difficultez, si j'en rencontre en lisant, je n'en
ronge pas mes ongles; je les laisse là, apres leur avoir fait une charge
ou deux. Si ce livre me fasche, j'en prens un autre. . . ." Now the
word *charge,* here a metaphor for attacking the difficulties of a text,
is frequent in the erotic imagery of the period. Is it a coincidence that
in the *b* text Montaigne inserts between these two sentences a passage
in which a whole series of words (the ones I have italicized) can be
interpreted in this sense?

> Si je *m'y plantois,* je m'y perdrois, et le temps: car j'ay un esprit
> primsautier. Ce que je ne voy de la premiere *charge,* je le voy
> moins en m'y obstinant. Je ne fay rien sans gayeté; et la contin-
> uation esblouït mon jugement, l'*attriste* et le *lasse.* Il faut que je le
> *retire* et que je l'y remette *à secousses:* tout ainsi que, pour juger du
> lustre de l'escarlatte, on nous ordonne de passer les yeux par-dessus,
> en la parcourant à diverses veuës, *soudaines, reprinses,* et *reiterées.*

There is an extraordinary profusion of analogy in this passage—
reading/attacking, reading/doing, reading/looking—and I see nothing unlikely in the additional analogy between *jugement* and a *mem-
bre* which Montaigne discusses freely in other essays. The *c* additions,

which concern the reading/looking analogy, attenuate the force of
this passage, but the tone of the *b* text seems to me obvious. Not that
there is any profound philosophical significance in this analogy, except that it forms part of Montaigne's constant plea for the equal
validity of all human activity—it is a joke, and a good one too. My
interpretation is confirmed by the next section of the *a* text, where he
mentions three writers well known for their interest in eroticism,
Boccaccio, Rabelais, and Jean Second, and says that "cette vieille ame
poisante ne se laisse plus chatouiller" by Ariosto and Ovid. The rest
of this essay interests us mainly for its information about Montaigne's
reading habits, but these first few pages contain some very typical
self-deprecation and *boutade*.

"Du dementir" (II, xviii; 1578–80, according to Villey) looks as
though it will treat the same subject as "Des menteurs," and to some
extent it does. The *a* text contains a close repetition of the earlier essay
("C'est un vilein vice que le mentir," p. 666), giving the same reason
("Nostre intelligence se conduisant par la seule voye de la parolle").
But most of the essay, especially in its final version, is an apology for
Montaigne's self-portrait, and thus it is much more like the later
essays than the earlier ones. It is this aspect of the essay which I should
like to examine, since Montaigne's attitude to his portrait of himself
is an important part of his whole bluff technique.

The *a* text makes it clear that "Du dementir" is a continuation of
the previous essay, "De la praesumption," in which he had also discussed truth, lying, memory, and himself. This essay was in turn a
continuation of "De la gloire," so the main subject of this group of
essays is the relationship between the public and private man, between
what others think of us and what we are. Montaigne uses himself as
an example of this whole problem and goes on to defend himself
against a charge of exhibitionism because he talks about himself so
much. This charge is almost certainly imaginary; it appears from most
contemporary judgments that Montaigne's readers liked his portrait of
himself. And while in II, xviii, the emphasis will be on the truth of

his portrait, in II, xvii, the emphasis is on its lack of presumption, a plea which obviously encourages him to depreciate his value as proof that he is not boasting.

He begins "Du dementir" with a willing admission that his life is not of great interest, since he is neither "rare" nor "fameux." He then asserts that he does not expect a wide public (p. 664); whereas others have undertaken their autobiography "pour y avoir trouvé le subject digne et riche; moy, au rebours, pour l'avoir trouvé si sterile et si maigre qu'il n'y peut eschoir soupçon d'ostentation." Clearly in this sentence *digne* and *riche* are ironic, since the authors who consider themselves so are by implication guilty of *ostentation*. This sentence is, in any case, not serious: if *digne* and *riche* are ironic, *sterile* and *maigre* are overapologetic. And if the next *a* paragraph, about his veneration for his ancestors, may be serious, the following one certainly is not. Montaigne makes a joke about his posterity, a joke about the printing of his book, and a joke about the possible practical uses of the *Essais*. The *c* text adds a French version of the Latin quotation in *a,* to make the bantering tone clear even to those readers who normally skip Latin quotations.

The following *a* sentence leads into the question of lying: "Mais, à qui croyrons nous parlant de soy, en une saison si gastée? veu qu'il en est peu, ou point, à qui nous puissions croire, parlant d'autruy, où il y a moins d'interest à mentir" (p. 666). Does this not invalidate the supposed "sincerity" of Montaigne at one blow? The rest of the essay attempts to prove that one can no longer distinguish truth from falsehood—the age is so corrupt that lying has become a virtue. So this first sentence appears to mean "Even if I do tell the truth, who will recognize it?" If Montaigne were really concerned about his self-portrait, one would expect him to pursue this aspect of the matter, but he does not, choosing to end the essay with a condemnation of lying and of the foolish laws of honor relative to *nos dementirs.* The implication may be that I, Montaigne, in contrast to the rest of my century, always tell the truth, but the *a* text of the essay seems to use the self-portrait theme, carried over from "De la praesumption," as an introduction to the lying theme, which is the main point of the essay.

The reason "Du dementir" is normally considered one of the more important self-portrait essays is that in the *c* text Montaigne added a long passage justifying his habit of self-portraiture (pp. 665–66). I think that some mistaken emphasis has been put on this passage, and I should like to examine it carefully. One's first impression on reading it is that Montaigne only ever writes about himself, that the main purpose of the essays is his self-portrait. This is simply not true; there is not one essay which is only about himself, and in most of the first two books he uses self-portraiture merely as illustration of whatever subject he is discussing.

Second, this passage is an answer not to a charge of insincerity but to a charge of wasting his time by writing about himself, and it is a simple enumeration of the reasons that he doesn't think he has wasted his time. These reasons are of different orders, and there is no logical development in their enumeration. One might list them as follows: (1) His portrait in the book has had a positive influence on his character. (2) He has assured a more thorough examination of himself, by writing down the results, than if he had simply thought or spoken about himself. (3) The task of writing has often been a diversion from gloomy thoughts. (4) The act of writing has helped him organize his thoughts. (5) The act of writing helps him remember what he thinks. (6) In the *Essais* he can condemn openly things he would not dare to in conversation, thereby providing *publique instruction.* (7) He reads with more care now that he is looking for quotations and arguments to appropriate.

Of these seven reasons, only the first two apply directly to his self-portrait in the *Essais;* the others apply to the book in general. So let us look more closely at reasons 1 and 2. To take 2 first, it says nothing about the self-portrait but only about the beneficial effects of self-examination. And the force of this is considerably attenuated by the next sentence ("Les plus delicieux plaisirs . . ."), which suggests that the most profound parts of one's personality cannot be recorded ("fuyent à laisser trace de soi"), in which case no self-portrait can be complete.

But the most interesting reason of them all is the first, which has also been the most discussed. What Montaigne appears to be saying is that his book has changed him. Does he mean that he has deliberately altered his character in order to conform to the self-portrait in the book? Probably not, although "le patron s'en est . . . aucunement formé soy-mesmes" could be so interpreted. Does he mean that by examining himself in the book, he has become more aware of his personality? Or more aware of his opinions? There is a substantial, to use Montaigne's word, difference here; is he talking about his character and habits, as "Me peignant pour autruy" would suggest, or rather about his view of life and the side he takes in any given issue? The text is, I think deliberately, vague, and as I have already mentioned, I cannot take literally the "livre consubstantiel à son autheur." [38] There is a plethora of analogy in these three sentences: portrait/moulded statue, portrait/painting, self-improvement(?)/painting, book/man/body, book/member of body. Are *all* these analogies to be taken seriously as statements about the nature of his book? The transition from "dead" analogies (*moulant, me peignant*) to the living analogy with substance is particularly interesting, since if one can just barely visualize a book as organic, growing and developing like a body, it is impossible so to visualize a painting, still less a moulded sculpture. Besides Montaigne wants to have it both ways— the self-portrait both is modeled on himself (this is what he maintains *ad infinitum* in the other essays) and models him (which is what he is underlining here).

A similar *c* passage in "De l'exercitation" (II, vi, 378), which is also a reply to the charge of presumption, refers even more clearly to the necessary artificiality of the self-portrait: "Il n'est description

[38] See above, pp. 116–17.

pareille en difficulté à la description de soy-mesmes, ny certes en utilité. Encore se faut-il testoner, encore se faut-il ordonner et renger pour sortir en place. Or je me pare sans cesse, car je me descris sans cesse." In the last two sentences of this paragraph the reflexive pronouns are ambiguous. There are three *personae* involved in any first-person narration: the author as person, the author as creator, and the representation of the author in the book. To which of them does Montaigne's *Encore se faut-il testoner* refer? To the portrait, which must be tidied up in order to please the reader, or to the author as person, who must be tidied up so that the portrait of him will please the reader? I cannot believe that Montaigne is unaware of this ambiguity, and the fact that he takes no pains to dissipate it is a further indication of a preference for ambiguity and mystification. This preference, though often essentially lighthearted, does not, of course, preclude an emphasis on the "moral" importance of what he is saying.

"Du dementir," then, short as it is, confirms the convictions gained from other essays in the first two books: Montaigne's thought is from the beginning extremely complex, and his main purpose is to draw attention to this complexity rather than to resolve it; his approach to his self-portrait is humorously self-deprecating and ambiguous; and it amuses him to shift the emphasis in successive additions to the same essay. Like "Des menteurs," "Du dementir" looks quite different in the final version—it now appears to be about the self-portrait rather than about lying. But, like "Des menteurs," it contained even in the first version complexities, ambiguities, and a basically humorous tone.

BOOK III

The essays of the last book are usually better known, and have certainly been more thoroughly discussed and analyzed, than those of the first two books. Are they really so different, so much more interesting? I hope to have shown already that this qualitative difference between the earlier and the later essays has been greatly exaggerated, but there is undoubtedly a difference; in what does it consist? Certainly not in subject matter or theme—almost no new subjects are discussed in the third book. Nor has Montaigne radically changed his mind on any subject except death. The essays have in general become longer, but only two of them, "De la vanité" and "De l'experience," are strikingly longer than any (except the "Apologie") in the other books.

The obvious differences in the Book III essays are artistic and structural. Montaigne does not talk much more about himself, but he does talk more about his book. Moreover, the individual essays stick more closely to their subjects than did the earlier ones, so that less effort is involved in following the train of thought. Most important, Montaigne is clearly much more conscious of the artistic structure and unity of the individual essay. He comments more often on the links between different parts of an essay, he places key words—"mots en un coing"—to mark the progression of his thought, and his use of analogy becomes more systematic and unifying. He still employs most of the bluff techniques we have discussed, but they are more closely incorporated into the structure of the essay. And this structure is itself very different. Not only are the later essays a great deal richer in imagery; they are orchestrated, so to speak, instead of arranged in layers via logical association. Nearly all of them discuss, as well as the specific subject matter, *all* of Montaigne's basic preoccupations: death, diversity, experience, *le masque, la parole,* himself, and his style. "Tout est dans tout," as Baraz says,[39] or as Montaigne himself puts it, "Les matieres se tiennent toutes enchesnées les unes aux autres" (III, v, 876). Each essay might stand by itself as a discussion of Montaigne's main interests. And these interests run through the essay like musical themes, recurring at intervals and often when least expected.

There are exceptions to this. In "De l'utile et de l'honneste" (III, i) Montagne is proceeding just as he did in the earlier essays with abstract titles—he is showing that the clichés about honor versus ex-

39 Baraz, *L'être et la connaissance*, p. 181.

pediency are based on muddled thinking. Not only are *l'utile* and *l'honneste* not always in opposition to one another, but they are radically different in nature, since *l'honneste* is one ("La voye de la verité est une et simple," p. 795), whereas expediency is multiple. Moreover, the "langage commun, qui faict difference entre les choses utiles et les honnestes" (p. 796) is often mistaken: "d'aucunes actions naturelles, non seulement utiles, mais necessaires, il les nomme deshonnestes et sales." Montaigne is not denying the existence of a distinction between *l'utile* and *l'honneste*—unlike *gloire* and *repentir,* they do exist and can be distinguished—but he is saying that the distinction is not always the superficial, cut-and-dried one made by most people. Montaigne is as fond of an antithesis as the next man, but it must be a valid one.

This essay sticks closely to its subject, and the tone is generally serious. Its unity is emphasized by the use, every page or so, of *utile* or *honneste,* to recall the subject to our attention, and by the quite explicit conclusion, which for once is found almost at the end of the essay: "On argumente mal *l'honnesteté* et la beauté d'une action par son *utilité,* et conclud on mal d'estimer que chacun y soit obligé si elle est *utile*" (p. 803: *b; my italics). The *c* text adds "et qu'elle soit *honneste* à chacun" after *obligé,* thereby reinforcing both the point Montaigne is making and the symmetry of the sentence. But Montaigne has not abandoned his technique of the final *boutade.* Did he perhaps feel that the whole essay was rather somber in tone? In any case, the *b* text adds a brief example of dubious judgment on this subject: marriage is *utile,* but the Church has proclaimed celibacy more *honneste,* and Montaigne finishes his essay with the words "comme nous assignons au haras les bestes qui sont de moindre estime." We need not suppose that he is degrading priests by comparing them to horses—he is simply ending this essay, as he has so many others, on a humorous note.

"Du repentir" is a continuation of "De l'utile et de l'honneste," as the story of the unrepentant thief makes clear. He considered his thieving "action des-honneste" (p. 812), but since his need made *l'utile* more important than *l'honneste,* he did not regret it. As we would expect from the title, Montaigne sets out to show us that what most people call repentance is not worthy of the name, that true repentance entails a complete change of heart. This is part of one of his main themes, the gulf between a man's inner nature and his outer mask, between "essence" and "apparence" (p. 813). Once again the whole essay is on one subject which is never lost sight of, the *c* text does not introduce a change of tone, and the air of moral instruction is readily apparent. The much-quoted "forme maistresse" passage (p. 811: *b*) looks like a deliberate contradiction of what he had said about his self-portrait in the first paragraph (pp. 804–5).

This essay, ostensibly on a traditional moral *topos,* is in fact yet another illustration of one of his favorite themes: words and things. "Repentance," as we use the word, is a mask, not a reality. In spite of the structure of the essay, which never ranges very far from the subject, he manages to refer at some length to himself, his book, moderation, old age, and Socrates, and he will do the same sort of thing in all the remaining essays. "De trois commerces" is about communication but contains an extended self-portrait, some moralizing on women, more on the mask, and a detailed description of his library. "De la diversion" discusses the passions in general and how to excite or appease them, our inability to concentrate ("nous pensons toujours ailleurs," p. 834; cf. the title of I, iii: "Nos affections s'emportent au dela de nous"), death, and the mask again.

"Sur des vers de Virgile," to which I shall return, is about many other things besides sex, and the bewildering variety of subjects in "Des coches" has received widely differing attempts at synthesis.[40] In this essay in particular it is difficult to emphasize one theme at the expense of the others—all of them combine into a musical whole. "De l'incommodité de la grandeur" is short and simple, a return to

---

[40] See an excellent analysis by R. A. Sayce, "Baroque Elements in Montaigne," *FS* VIII (1954), 1–16; and an impertinent and largely irrelevant reply to Sayce by R. Etiemble, "Sens et structure dans un essai de Montaigne," *CAIEF* XIV (1962), 263–74.

the manner of the early essays, but "De l'art de conferer," already discussed, is much more complex.[41] Ostensibly on communication again, like "De trois commerces," and specifically on the rules of formal debate, it has a great deal to say about all sorts of subjects, including presumption, tyranny, and history. However, whereas in "Des coches" the transition from one subject to the next was deliberately disconcerting, and all themes were apparently of equal value, here we definitely have minor themes subordinated to, and dependent upon, the main one. It seems that Montaigne in Book III is deliberately experimenting with different types of structure.

I have already discussed some aspects of "De la vanité" and have suggested that its tone is more lighthearted than critics have allowed.[42] The title is at least partially a joke, since one of the meanings of *vanité* is "nothing," and the structure of the essay illustrates the point I made earlier about "marqueterie mal jointe."[43] The apparent "digressions" on traveling and his style create an artificial impression of disjointedness; in fact, of course, they are not digressions at all. The subject of the essay is not, obviously, "nothing" but, rather, the analogy man's life/book/journey, and the structure is not *mal jointe* but quite harmonious.

"De mesnager sa volonté" is largely what it appears to be, a recommendation of the golden mean in public and private affairs, but as usual it takes in many other subjects as it goes. "Des boyteux" is probably intended to be about sorcery but also discusses human reason, causes, lying, judgment, and illusion.[44] And there is no need to underline the range of subjects covered in "De la phisionomie" and "De l'experience."

But in all these essays, with the possible exception of "Des coches," an impression of harmony prevails. Has Montaigne abandoned bluff?

[41] See above, p. 121.
[42] See above, p. 118.
[43] See above, p. 123 and note 22.
[44] See Alan M. Boase, "Montaigne et la sorcellerie," *BHR* II (1935), 402–21.

Has he decided to make of each essay an autonomous work of art, differently orchestrated from the others but definitely possessing its own internal harmony? I think rather that he is bluffing as much as ever, but much more subtly—so subtly, in fact, that a very close scrutiny of the text is required to find the disconcerting aspects which formerly leaped to the eye. As an example of this, I should like to examine "Sur des vers de Virgile." What is Montaigne doing in this essay, and is it the same as what he says he is doing?

The title of the essay is another joke—who could possibly guess that of all the lines Virgil wrote, Montaigne happens to be thinking of the passage from *Aeneid,* VIII, which he will quote on p. 849? It is, in fact, fairly clear by p. 847 that the main subject of the essay is sex, but the reader of the first few pages has no idea of this and thus no idea why Montaigne begins with a plea for gaiety to offset the somberness of old age. He begins, in fact, with excuses for treating a frivolous and scabrous subject, long before he mentions what the subject is. And these excuses vary from the lighthearted to the dishonest. The first is that old age needs some light relief if it is not to suffer from "l'excez . . . de la severité" (p. 841); the second is that "je me suis ordonné d'oser dire tout ce que j'ose faire" (p. 845) —the implication being that since frankness and sincerity set a good example, there is some kind of moral utility in explicit discussion of sex. This is clearly not serious and, moreover, not true. The Latin quotations are erotic but not explicit, and in French Montaigne "dares to say" a great deal less than Rabelais, Des Périers, Nicholas de Troyes, or Brantôme. The third excuse is that writing about sex will give him the intimate access to women which he can no longer have in person because of his age (p. 847).

We have a very subtle mixture, in these first few pages, of seriousness and lightheartedness. The regret for old age is no doubt serious, as is the dislike of gloomy moralizing and the desire for frankness. But the references to sex and women are largely lighthearted, and there is a suggestion, nowhere formulated in so many words, that Montaigne's main reason for writing about sex is that he enjoys talking about it. Nothing, certainly, could be more "natural."

I suggest that he has two other major reasons for writing this essay, nowhere explicitly stated but obvious from a brief consideration of some of Montaigne's sources. I have mentioned already (see above, p. 125) Montaigne's reference to Plato's *Phaedrus* as "mi party d'une fantastique bigarrure, le devant à l'amour, tout le bas à la rhetorique" (III, ix, 994). This description would fit "Sur des vers de Virgile" remarkably well, always granting that Montaigne is discussing many more subjects than Plato. It also draws our attention to the *Phaedrus* as a possible source. Montaigne's judgment is quite fair—Plato's dialogue is half on love and half on rhetoric, and the transition from one to the other is rather brusque (section XXXIX), whereas Montaigne's own transition from sex to language via poetry is extremely smooth (pp. 872–73). But the main difference is, of course, that Plato is talking about love as he understands it: desire for ultimate good, the fourth and most divine fury, which transcends earthly beauty altogether. Physical desire is hardly in question, whereas for Montaigne it is the whole question.

Plato's concept of human love is, in any case, homosexual, which brings me to another very interesting source which Montaigne definitely used for this essay, Plutarch's treatise *On Love*. This is an obvious imitation of a Platonic dialogue, complete with story framework, but one of the main points discussed is precisely homosexual versus heterosexual love. Plutarch is apparently in favor of marriage, but one wonders why Montaigne does not even mention homosexuality. From prudence, in view of the notorious mores of Henri III? Or because love between men is part of the neo-Platonic tradition which he is implicitly and explicitly combating in this essay?

For there is no doubt that "Sur des vers de Virgile" reads like a systematic refutation of Plato and Plutarch. No mention of the soul, which is an essential subject in the *Phaedrus* and *On Love;* a detailed discussion of the physical side of love and a clear rejection of any aspiration to transcend it: "Mon page fait l'amour et l'entend. Lisez luy Leon Hébreu et Ficin [the two major exponents of the neo-Platonic school of love]: on parle de luy, de ses pensées et de ses actions, et si [= pourtant] il n'y entend rien" (p. 874).

The essential aspects of love, for Plato and Plutarch, are for Montaigne artificial trappings masking the reality, which he expresses crudely enough: "*b*) je trouve apres tout que l'amour n'est autre chose que la soif de cette jouyssance *c*) en un subject desiré, ny Venus autre chose que le plaisir à descharger ses vases" (p. 877). Was La Rochefoucauld thinking of this passage when he wrote his maxim 68? In any case, it states plainly an attitude directly opposed to the first part of the *Phaedrus*.

And what about the second part? Is Montaigne not as much against rhetoric as he is against Platonic love? On p. 873 he makes the transition from sex to language via another quotation, from Lucretius this time. This is one of the rare examples in the *Essais* of what we would call "literary criticism," and Friedrich regards it as an important definition of Montaigne's own style. What Montaigne is advocating is simplicity and words that perfectly express thought, as opposed to "menues pointes et allusions verballes." He does not state specifically that he is opposing the whole rhetorical tradition from Cicero to Ramus, but this impression emerges very strongly from the passage. He uses four of the technical terms belonging to this tradition—*eloquence, jugement, figures,* and *invention*—and makes a strong distinction between *bien dire,* which is the classic definition of rhetoric, and *bien penser,* which is his aim. I would say, then, that this whole essay is basically an anti-*Phaedrus:* half of it refuting Platonic love as a concept and the other half undermining Platonic rhetoric as a discipline.

Of course, this is only a starting point. The essay is extremely complex and very different in structure from "Des coches," for instance, which immediately follows it. A diagram could be drawn of it in the form of a wheel (an analogy made by many critics for the *Essais*), with sex as the hub and the other subjects arranged around the rim, connected by spokes to the hub. The most important of these subjects, and their connection with the central subject of sex, are as follows:

1) old age, because old men are impotent, inclined to somberness, and in need of cheering up;

2) sincerity, because most people dare not talk about sex;

3) marriage, because sex in marriage must be kept within strict bounds (cf. I, xxx);

4) poetry, because sex therein is more exciting than in real life;

5) *la volonté,* because a jealous husband can control his wife's actions but not her desires;

6) rhetoric, via plain-speaking, an important aspect of sincerity;

7) his book, via rhetoric and because his book is about him and sex concerns him;

8) custom, because of the entertaining diversity of sexual customs and the question of the education of women;

9) *la condition humaine,* of which sex is an essential part which must not be ignored;

10) *la vanité,* because in love we concentrate on superfluous matters and forget, or hide, the essential;

11) *le masque,* via sincerity, *vanité,* and rhetoric;

12) old age again, because old men are still men, but love is suitable only for youth;

13) body and soul, because both are necessary for love—a final dig at the neo-Platonic emphasis on soul.

In spite of Montaigne's denigrating remarks at the end—"Pour finir ce notable commentaire, qui m'est eschappé d'un flux de caquet, flux impetueux par fois et nuisible . . ." (p. 897)—this essay has an almost circular construction which is quite easy to follow. All the subjects just enumerated are connected to the central subject of sex, and most of them are also interconnected. The first and last major subjects are both old age, and the second and penultimate both sincerity or *essence* versus *apparence,* so that Montaigne very nearly brings his essay back to its starting point. Not quite, however—he adds some apparently random reflections at the end to spoil the symmetry. At the same time symmetry is emphasized by another technique very common in Book III—the frequent recalling of a subject related to the one he is actually discussing. For instance, in the passage on the education of women he tells the story of his daughter's governess, who forbade her to read the word *fouteau* (p. 856). This recalls immediately the *parole* theme and the important point that our attitude to sex is mainly "superstition verbale" (p. 888).

Like many other essays, then, this one is much more structured than it appears, another disconcerting aspect. A very important third aspect is the question of tone. I have mentioned several essays which end lightheartedly; this one, on the contrary, begins lightheartedly and becomes more and more serious as it proceeds. The most probable reason for this is that Montaigne did not realize, when he began to write, quite how "central" a subject sex would turn out to be. So we find, as in Rabelais, curious shifts of tone from tongue-in-cheek to serious. Parts of the long central section on marriage (pp. 849–72) look like an *éloge* or *blason* of a member which is normally not so dignified; but there is no reason to doubt the serious import of remarks like "nous estimons à vice nostre estre" (p. 879).

What, then, are we to make of the plea for moderation in marital intercourse (pp. 849–58)? Montaigne had already expressed the same point of view in "De la moderation" (I, xxx), which is already an enigma (see above, p. 139). Does he really believe that one should not overexcite one's wife? It is, of course, possible that he does believe it, but he also discusses at length the way women are brought up and the unrealistic double standard which men impose upon them ("Nous . . . les voulons . . . et chaudes et froides," p. 855). At the end of the essay he states that the differences between men and women are mainly due to "l'institution et l'usage" (p. 897). So we have here a mixture of feminist and antifeminist (from a modern point of view) opinions, an exposé of both sides of the *querelle des femmes*, with no positive evidence as to Montaigne's own conclusion.

I would suggest that this essay contains nearly all of the "bluff" aspects of Montaigne which have been discussed in this chapter, and that a résumé of these aspects makes a good conclusion to my argument. We have so far noted the following:

1) the title, which looks like a guessing game;

2) the introduction, which is puzzling (because the subject has not yet been announced) and misleading;

3) Montaigne's actual reasons for writing the essay are not the reasons he gives;

4) the subjects of sex and rhetoric appear at first sight totally unconnected;

5) the structure is more symmetrical and conscious than Montaigne admits;

6) the shifts in tone are not only disconcerting but profoundly ambiguous.

This is a good beginning, but there is far more.

7) One of the main interests of sex as a subject is that our attitude toward it is ambiguous. Montaigne is here criticizing ambiguity on the moral plane, while as usual indulging in it on the intellectual plane and actually enjoying it on the aesthetic plane (diversity of sexual customs, irrelevance of treating courtesans as though they were virgins). As noted at the beginning of this chapter, this conscious interweaving of frames of reference is a major component in Montaigne's art of bluff.

8) Nearly all of the subjects treated give rise to contradictions or subsidiary paradoxes. Thus under sincerity he treats the problem of a choice between two vices, such as that Origen had to make (p. 846). Under marriage arise several paradoxes: women are more lustful than men, but they have to be chaste and men don't (p. 854); chastity is more difficult than the "positive" virtues: "Il n'y poinct de faire plus espineux qu'est ce non faire, ny plus actif" (p. 861); cuckoldry is not

necessarily a disaster (p. 870)—this is, of course, a traditional *topos*.

9) Montaigne thoroughly enjoys emphasizing the ridiculous aspects of desire: "*b*) ce visage enflammé de fureur et de cruauté au plus doux effect de l'amour . . . *c*) et qu'on aye logé peslemesle nos delices et nos ordures ensemble, *b*) et que la supreme volupté aye du transy et du plaintif comme la douleur" (p. 877). In the same section he develops other paradoxes: that we need clothing and outward ceremony to excite desire (pp. 880–81), whereas elsewhere he deplores any mask in connection with sex; that possession destroys desire (p. 881); or that "chacun fuit à le voir naistre, chacun suit à le voir mourir" (p. 878).

10) He emphasizes, here as elsewhere, the paradoxical and playful aspects of his writing. As noted earlier in this chapter, he gives a list of reproaches that have been leveled at his book, including "*b*) Voilà un discours paradoxe. En voilà un trop fol. *c*) Tu te joues souvent" (p. 875), and a page later he states, "*b*) Et ce que j'auray pris à dire en battellant et en me moquant, je le diray lendemain serieusement. . . . Tout argument m'est egallement fertile . . . [les] plus profondes resveries [de mon ame], plus folles et qui me plaisent le mieux. . . ."

11) Every few pages a minor paradox, not essential to the argument but apparently slipped in in passing, reminds us of his basic preoccupation. Some examples: "D'une humanité à la verité plus qu'humaine!" (p. 864); "les mesmes causes qui servoient de fondement à la bienvueillance servent de fondement de hayne capitale" (p. 865); "les peintres ombragent leur ouvrage, pour luy donner plus de lustre" (p. 880); "Et Thrasonidez, jeune homme grec, fut si amoureux de son amour, qu'il refusa . . . d'en jouyr" (p. 881); "Periander fit plus monstrueusement, qui estendist l'affection conjugale (plus reiglée et legitime) à la jouyssance de Melissa, sa femme trespassée" (p. 882); "on peut oser plus aysément ce que personne ne pense que vous oserez, qui devient facile par sa difficulté" (p. 890).

By comparing this essay with the Book I chapters analyzed earlier, we can see how Montaigne has changed and also to what extent he remains the same. He is still fascinated by complex and ambiguous subjects and the complex and ambiguous thought processes we use to deal with them, and he delights just as much in jokes, puns, antitheses, and paradoxes. But whereas in the first two books these shock techniques were obviously disconcerting, in the last book they are more subtly so. They have become part of the fabric of the essay to such an extent that we barely notice them unless, as I have tried to do in this chapter, we set out deliberately to look for them. The shock techniques which Rabelais delighted in for their own sake have become, in Montaigne's last essays, fused into an art of bluff. My analysis of "Sur des vers de Virgile" was intended to underline some of the ways in which this art works, but to do it full justice would require a whole book devoted to each essay. Let me return for a moment to the distinction between moral, intellectual, and aesthetic planes which I suggested at the beginning of this chapter. In the final essays Montaigne is denouncing or exploiting ambiguity and paradox on each level; willfully mingling the levels; describing incoherent thought processes by means of a coherent metaphorical structure; decorating each point as he goes along with irrelevant, as well as relevant, minor paradoxes and ambiguities; and, perhaps most remarkable of all, using ambiguity himself, in a constantly entertaining manner, to make us aware and ashamed of our own ambiguity in thought and action.

We have here, it seems to me, one of the most startling tours de force in the whole of French literature. Intellectually Montaigne is just as destructive as he was in Book I, and morally he is just as dogmatic. He should by rights be either depressing us by showing up our faults or annoying us by his firm statements on moral conduct. And yet, so far from doing either of these things, he has above all given us pleasure. We have come to know a man, complex certainly but never contradictory, who is essentially a sympathetic character; we have been made to rethink a good many of our preconceived ideas;

and we have been both stimulated and satisfied by a great work of literature. After reading a single essay in Book I or II we remained unsatisfied, realizing that we have been given just one facet of a many-faceted talent. But a Book III essay is a work of art in itself and to a large extent self-sufficient. From "Sur des vers de Virgile" we have learned a great deal about Montaigne the man and the intellectual, and about what he thinks is wrong with us as men and as intellectuals. We have been entertained by his erudition, wit, and humor and aesthetically satisfied by the structure and style of his essay. He has managed, in fact, simultaneously to disconcert and please us, and in this sense we can characterize his art as the art of bluff.

Afterword

This book has no conclusion. It was intended as a study, necessarily one-sided in its emphasis, of an aspect of the French Renaissance which has, to my mind, been largely ignored by most critics. I am not for a moment suggesting that the view of Rabelais and Montaigne outlined here supersedes or excludes other views. On the contrary, I am convinced that there is not, and never will be, a definitive answer to the question, "What makes them great writers?" The very partial answer suggested in these pages is meant, as I stated in my first chapter, mainly to redress a balance. There has been too much critical emphasis on unifying elements in Rabelais and Montaigne, so to counteract this emphasis, I have underlined the various techniques of bluff. But this is not counter-argument for its own sake. If the Renaissance has an aesthetic outlook, it lies precisely here, in an emphasis on complexity, contradiction, and diversity in all domains. The richness and variety of French Renaissance literature is itself evidence of this. For whatever combination of reasons, France is not yet ready for Classicism, and the "regular" genres of the age—Jodelle's *Cléopâtre,* Ronsard's *Franciade*—are failures. The successes, for contemporary readers as for us, are precisely the unclassifiable nongenres: Rabelais's rambling pseudo-epic, Montaigne's "essays" of his judgment and personality.

Nor am I implying any "evolution," in the accepted sense of the word, between Rabelais and Montaigne. They provide two different examples of the Renaissance preoccupation with bluff. Rabelais concentrates on shocking us and making us laugh, and although his interest in and exploitation of paradox and ambiguity clearly increases from book to book, he shows no desire even in the last one to come to any conclusions. He enjoys presenting riddles and never bothers to give us the answers. Montaigne, on the other hand, seems to have a more synthetic mind, judging by the gradual absorption of bluff techniques into an art form in the later essays. I see no reason to connect this tendency of Montaigne's with his closeness in time to the seventeenth century, and, indeed, Rabelais is probably the more "baroque" of the two.

I hope, then, that this study has raised some fruitful questions for further research to elucidate. It has certainly raised in my mind many questions which I cannot answer. The intellectual background discussed in Chapter I does not satisfactorily explain the prevalence of bluff techniques at this time; what other reasons are there? Where did Rabelais and Montaigne acquire their deep suspicion of the spoken word and its uses? These questions and many others await further investigation. If this book has convinced you that paradox and ambiguity are important explanatory factors in the work of Rabelais and Montaigne, as of the century in general, then it has amply achieved its purpose.

Selected Bibliography

I. WORKS ON RABELAIS

Bakhtin, Mikhail. *Rabelais and His World.* Tr. Helene Iswolsky. Cambridge, Mass.: M.I.T. Press, 1968.

Bowen, Barbara. "Rabelais and the Comedy of the Spoken Word." *MLR* LXIII (1968), 575–80.

Brault, G. J. "'Ung abysme de science': On the Interpretation of Gargantua's Letter to Pantagruel." *BHR* XXVIII (1966), 615–32.

Butor, Michel. "La faim et la soif." *Critique* (Oct. 1968), pp. 827–54.

Coleman, Dorothy. "The Prologues of Rabelais." *MLR* LXII (1967), 407–19.

Gray, Floyd. "Ambiguity and Point of View in the Prologue to *Gargantua*." *RR* LVI (1965), 12–21.

———. "Structure and Meaning in the Prologue to the *Tiers livre*." *L'Esprit Créateur,* III, no. 2 (Summer 1963), 57–62.

Guiton, Jean. "Le mythe des paroles gelées." *RR* XXXI (1940), 3–15.

Kaiser, Walter. *Praisers of Folly: Erasmus, Rabelais, Shakespeare.* Cambridge, Mass.: Harvard University Press, 1963.

Krailsheimer, A. J. *Rabelais and the Franciscans.* Oxford: Clarendon Press, 1963.

Lebègue, Raymond. "Rabelaesiana." *BHR* X (1948), 159–68.

———. "Rabelais, the Last of the French Erasmians." *Journal of the Warburg and Courtauld Institute* XII (1949), 91–100.

Marichal, Robert. "L'attitude de Rabelais devant le néoplatonisme et l'italianisme." In *François Rabelais: ouvrage publié pour le 4e centenaire de sa mort.* T.H.R., VII, 120–30. Geneva: Droz, 1953.

Paris, Jean. *Rabelais au futur.* Paris: Seuil, 1970.

Saulnier, V.-L. *Le dessein de Rabelais.* Paris: S.E.D.E.S., 1957.

———. "Pantagruel au large de Ganabin ou la peur de Panurge." *BHR* XVI (1954), 58–81.

———. "Le silence de Rabelais et le mythe des paroles gelées." In *François Rabelais: ouvrage publié pour le 4e centenaire de sa mort.* T.H.R., VII, 233–47. Geneva: Droz, 1953.

Screech, M. A. "The Death of Pan and Heroes." *BHR* XVII (1955), 36–55.

———. *L'évangélisme de Rabelais.* T.H.R., vol. XXXII; *Etudes Rabelaisiennes,* vol. II. Geneva: Droz, 1959.

———. *The Rabelaisian Marriage.* London: Arnold, 1958.

———. "The Sense of Rabelais' *Enigme en prophétie.*" *BHR* XVIII (1956), 392–404.

———. "Some Stoic Elements in Rabelais' Religious Thought." T.H.R., vols. XXIII–XXIV; *Etudes Rabelaisiennes,* I, 73–97. Geneva: Droz, 1956.

Spitzer, Leo. "Le prétendu réalisme de Rabelais." *MP* XXXVII (1939–40), 139–50.

———. "Rabelais et les rabelaisants." *SFr* XII (Sept.–Dec. 1960), 401–23.

Tetel, Marcel. *Etude sur le comique de Rabelais.* Biblioteca dell'*Archivum Romanicum,* ser. I, vol. LXIX. Florence: L. S. Olschki, 1964.

II. WORKS ON MONTAIGNE

Ballaguy, Paul. "La sincérité de Montaigne." *Mercure de France* (July–Aug. 1933), pp. 547–75.

Baraz, Michael. *L'être et la connaissance selon Montaigne.* Paris: Corti, 1968.

Bowen, Barbara. "What Does Montaigne Mean by *marqueterie?*" *SP* LXVII (1970), 147–55.

Bowman, Frank Paul. *Montaigne: Essays.* London: Arnold, 1965.

Buffum, Imbrie. *Studies in the Baroque from Montaigne to Rotrou.* New Haven, Conn.: Yale University Press, 1957.

Butor, Michel. *Essais sur les Essais.* Paris: Gallimard, 1968.

Clark, C. E. "Seneca's Letters to Lucilius as a Source of Some of Montaigne's Imagery." *BHR* XXX (1968), 250–66.

Dresden, S. "Le dilettantisme de Montaigne." *BHR* XV (1953), 45–56.

Frame, Donald. *Montaigne, a Biography.* New York: Harcourt, Brace, and World, 1965.

Françon, Marcel. "La chronologie des *Essais* de 1580." *Symposium* VIII (1954), 262–68.

Friedrich, Hugo. *Montaigne.* Tr. Robert Rovini. Paris: Gallimard, 1968.

Genz, Henry E. "Compositional Form in Montaigne's *Essais* and the Self-Portrait." *Kentucky Foreign Language Quarterly* X (1963), 133–39.

Gray, Floyd. *Le style de Montaigne.* Paris: Nizet, 1958.

———. "The Unity of Montaigne in the *Essais.*" *MLQ* XXII (1961), 79–86.

Hallie, Philip. *The Scar of Montaigne: An Essay in Personal Philosophy.* Middletown, Conn.: Wesleyan University Press, 1966.

Holyoake, S. J. "Further Reflections on Montaigne and the Concept of the Imagination." *BHR* XXXI (1969), 495–523.

———. "The Idea of *jugement* in Montaigne." *MLR* LXIII (1968), 340–51.

Parslow, Morris. "Montaigne's Composition: A Study of the Structure of the Essays of the Third Book." Ph.D. diss., Princeton University, 1954.

Porteau, Paul. *Montaigne et la vie pédagogique de son temps.* Paris: Droz, 1935.

Sayce, R. A. "Baroque Elements in Montaigne." *FS* VIII (1954), 1–16.

———. "Montaigne et la peinture du passage." *SRLF* IV (1963), 11–59.

———. "L'ordre des *Essais* de Montaigne." *BHR* XVIII (1956), 7–22.

Starobinski, Jean. "Montaigne en mouvement." *NRF* (Jan.–Mar. 1960), pp. 16–22, 254–66.

Strowski, Fortunat. *Montaigne.* 2nd ed. Paris: Alcan, 1931.

Thibaudet, Albert. *Montaigne, texte établi par Floyd Gray d'après les notes manuscrites.* Paris: Gallimard, 1963.

Traeger, Wolf E. *Aufbau und Gedankenführung in Montaignes Essais.* Heidelberg: C. Winter, 1961.

III. OTHER RENAISSANCE WRITERS

Agrippa, Cornelius. *Déclamation sur l'incertitude, vanité et abus des sciences.* Tr. Louis Turquet de Mayerne. Paris, 1582.

Boaystuau, P. *Le theatre du monde.* Antwerp, 1570.

Cassirer, E., P. O. Kristeller, and J. H. Randall, Jr., eds. *The Renaissance Philosophy of Man.* Chicago: University of Chicago Press, 1948.

The Colloquies of Erasmus: A New Translation. Tr. Craig R. Thompson. Chicago: University of Chicago Press, 1965.

Corrozet, Gilles. *Hécatomgraphie.* Paris: Champion, 1905.

De Brués, Guy. *Les dialogues . . . contre les nouveaux académiciens, que tout ne consiste point en opinion* (1557). Ed. Panos Paul Morphos. Baltimore: Johns Hopkins Press, 1953.

Desiderii Erasmi Roterodami opera omnia . . . tomus secundus, complectens adagia. Leiden, 1703; republished, London: Gregg Press, 1962.

Des Périers, Bonaventure. *Cymbalum mundi.* Ed. Peter H. Nurse. 2nd ed. Manchester: Manchester University Press, 1967.

Les dialogues de Jacques Tahureau gentilhomme du Mans. Ed. F. Conscience. Paris, 1870.

Du Bellay, Joachim. *Les regrets et autres oeuvres poëtiques.* Ed. J. Jolliffe and M. A. Screech. T.L.F. Geneva: Droz, 1966.

Erasmus, Desiderius. *The Praise of Folly.* Tr. Hoyt H. Hudson. Princeton, N.J.: Princeton University Press, 1941.

Estienne, Henri. *Deux dialogues du nouveau langage françois italianizé.* Ed. P. Ristelhuber. 2 vols. Paris, 1885.

Folengo, Theophile. *Histoire Maccaronique de Merlin Coccaïe.* Ed. Brunet and Jacob. Paris, 1876.

Lando, Ortensio. *Paradossi.* Lione, 1543.

La Ramée (Ramus), Pierre de. *Dialectique* (1555). Ed. Michel Dassonville. T.H.R., vol. LXVII. Geneva: Droz, 1964.

Le Caron, Loys. *Les dialogues.* Paris, 1556.

Navarre, Marguerite de. *L'heptaméron.* Ed. Michel François. Paris: Garnier, n.d.

Palissy, Bernard. *Les oeuvres.* Ed. Anatole France. Paris, 1880.

Phillips, Margaret Mann. *The "Adages" of Erasmus: A Study with Translations.* Cambridge: Cambridge University Press, 1964.

Rickard, Peter. *La langue française au seizième siècle.* Cambridge: Cambridge University Press, 1968. (Anthology of Renaissance texts.)

Schmidt, A.-M. *Poètes du XVIe siècle.* Paris: Bibliothèque de la Pléiade, 1953.

Sponde, Jean de. *Poésies.* Ed. François Ruchon and Alan Boase. Geneva: P. Cailler, 1949.

The Universe of Pontus de Tyard: A Critical Edition of L'univers. Ed. John C. Lapp. Ithaca, N.Y.: Cornell University Press, 1950.

IV. GENERAL WORKS

Allen, Don Cameron. *Image and Meaning: Metaphoric Traditions in Renaissance Poetry.* Baltimore: Johns Hopkins Press, 1960.

Boas, George. *The Happy Beast in French Thought of the Seventeenth Century.* Baltimore: Johns Hopkins Press, 1933.

Colie, Rosalie L. *Paradoxia Epidemica: The Renaissance Tradition of Paradox.* Princeton, N.J.: Princeton University Press, 1966.

Condeescu, N. N. "Le paradoxe bernesque dans la littérature française de la Renaissance." *BRP* II (1963), 27–51.

Crane, William G. *Wit and Rhetoric in the Renaissance: The Formal Basis of Elizabethan Prose Style.* New York: Columbia University Press, 1937.

Curtius, Ernst Robert. *European Literature and the Latin Middle Ages.* Tr. Willard R. Trask. New York: Harper and Row, 1963.

Dubois, Claude-Gilbert. "Autour d'un sonnet de Sponde: recherche de l'élément baroque." *L'Information Littéraire* (Mar.-Apr. 1967), pp. 86–92.

Empson, William. *Seven Types of Ambiguity.* New York: New Directions, n.d.

Febvre, Lucien. *Le problème de l'incroyance au XVIe siècle. La religion de Rabelais.* Paris: Michel, 1942.

Malloch, A. E. "The Techniques and Function of the Renaissance Paradox." *SP* LIII (1956), 191–203.

Ong, W. J. *Ramus, Method and the Decay of Dialogue: From the Art of Discourse to the Art of Reason.* Cambridge, Mass.: Harvard University Press, 1958.

Rice, Warner G. "The *Paradossi* of Ortensio Lando." In *Essays and Studies in English and Comparative Literature by Members of the English Department of the University of Michigan,* pp. 59–74. Ann Arbor: University of Michigan Press, 1932.

Saulnier, V.-L. "Proverbe et paradoxe du XVe au XVIe siècle. Un aspect majeur de l'antithèse: Moyen Age–Renaissance." In *Pensée humaniste et tradition chrétienne aux XVe et XVIe siècles.* Colloques Internationaux du C.N.R.S. Paris: C.N.R.S., 1950.

―――. "Le sens du *Cymbalum mundi* de Bonaventure Des Périers." *BHR* XIII (1951), 43–69, 137–71.

Sister M. Geraldine, C.S.J. "Erasmus and the Tradition of Paradox." *SP* LXI (1964), 41–63.